FOUNTAIN SQUARE AND THE GENIUS *of* WATER

THE HEART OF CINCINNATI

GREGORY PARKER ROGERS

Charleston London
THE History PRESS

Published by The History Press
Charleston, SC 29403
www.historypress.net

Cover photo courtesy of J. Miles Wolfe.

First published 2013

Manufactured in the United States

ISBN 978.1.60949.297.7

Library of Congress CIP data applied for.

For Roger A. Weber and J. Alan Lips

Contents

FOREWORD

Greg Rogers's new book, *Fountain Square and the Genius of Water: The Heart of Cincinnati*, provides an insightful history and perspective of the Tyler Davidson Fountain and the surrounding area at various times in the city's history. We learn how the city's stewards thought about Fountain Square and how they continuously focused the most noteworthy and accomplished designers, consultants and workers of the time on Fountain Square. Concerns such as the location of the fountain, pedestrian access to the square, amenities and visitor experience were constantly improved and updated to meet the needs of the day.

In addition to learning more about Fountain Square, our region's "living room," readers will get a sense of the dynamic life of a city. We see great civic events—celebration, controversy and mourning—take place at Fountain Square. We see the transformation from a focus on public transportation to the automobile to a pedestrian urban experience (and back to public transportation again). Fountain Square has always been a special destination, and Cincinnatians continue to treat it with the priority and respect it deserves.

My aunt, now in her eighties, recalls her mother returning from a visit to Fountain Square in the 1940s with news of the day from the people she would meet there. It nurtured an important sense of community. Today everyone can participate in lunchtime concerts, weekend movies, winter ice-skating and holiday events. Everyone wants to meet at Fountain Square...and always has.

Fountain Square is one of the most important pieces of real estate in southwest Ohio. How do I know? The evidence of this is the three overflowing boxes of meeting notes, stakeholder comments and consultant reports in my office from the 2006 renovation of Fountain Square. There were countless meetings and input sessions, passionate and vigorous debates and benchmarking trips to other cities. Along with several Downtown Cincinnati Inc. (DCI) board members, I was honored to participate in the Fountain Square Working Group, led by Jim Zimmerman, CEO of Federated Department Stores (now Macy's Inc.), for the Cincinnati Center City Development Corporation (3CDC). 3CDC, a nonprofit real estate development and finance organization, managed the renovation. There was a great investment of time, expertise and treasure to make sure the "new" Fountain Square was the best possible.

Why? Greg's book helps to answer this question by showing how Fountain Square and the surrounding area have always been iconic to Cincinnati. How Fountain Square and the surrounding area look, feel and operate plays a vital role in our ability to attract and retain the best and the brightest. It must be beautiful and well planned, secure and immaculately maintained. It must be vibrant, flexible and attractive for a multitude of uses.

The vision for Fountain Square's renovation was to "transform Fountain Square as the city's civic and retail heart." There were three elements: create a world-class public space at the core; create high-value retail, residential and commercial real estate; and be a catalyst for development throughout the center of the city.

Less than ten years later, we are seeing this vision realized. Thanks to the remarkable work of 3CDC, Fountain Square is an attractive and vibrant public space. Thanks to the vision and investment of nearby property owners, we now have new and revitalized businesses like Tiffany & Co., Palomino, Rock Bottom Brewery, Jos. A. Bank, Macy's and Saks Fifth Avenue. Many nearby, locally owned businesses are also thriving, such as Batsakes Hat Shop, Hunt Club Clothiers and Appointments. We see the just-opened 21c Museum Hotel and exciting new residential development. "Selling" a view of the re-energized Fountain Square has convinced many firms with offices overlooking the Square to invest and recommit to downtown, ensuring the economic importance of our city center for years to come. The renaissance has expanded beyond Fountain Square and now reaches the Ohio Riverfront, Over-the-Rhine and Pendleton with developments such as the Horseshoe Casino, The Banks, dunnhumby headquarters, Great American Tower at Queen City Square and many more investments throughout the city and region.

Everyone who has had the opportunity to be a part of the stewardship of Fountain Square—designers, city workers, construction workers, facility managers, planners and the DCI/Fountain Square Ambassadors—feels a special sense of pride. They have indeed been part of an important and special project.

It has been an honor to be a steward of Fountain Square, and I am delighted this book provides a rich and information-packed history of how the most important real estate in our region has evolved to meet the needs of the times.

DAVID GINSBURG
President and Chief Executive Officer, Downtown Cincinnati Inc.
January 2013

Acknowledgements

For those of us who grew up in Centerville, Ohio, in the 1970s, Cincinnati was the "big city." Fountain Square was then and is still today the focal point of Cincinnati. No trip to downtown then or now was complete without a visit to take in the sight of the fountain, which is the first and oldest public fountain of note in the United States.

I was very fortunate after I graduated from law school in Atlanta to be able to move anywhere in the country that I wished. I chose to come to my "big city" of Cincinnati, and I chose to join the law firm of Taft Stettinius & Hollister, whose offices overlook Fountain Square at the corner of Fifth and Walnut Streets in the U.S. Bank Tower. Both decisions were very good ones for me. Taft has been my professional home for more than half my life—almost twenty-five years—and I am privileged to co-chair the Labor and Employment Law Department. Cincinnati, my adopted hometown, was a very good choice for me.

History has long been a passion for me. I got connected with The History Press a few years ago when the folks there asked me to write a book about the history of my Cincinnati neighborhood, Hyde Park. I did that and published a book in 2010, *Cincinnati's Hyde Park: A Queen City Gem*. That book did well enough that I decided to write this second book about the fountain outside my office window—the Genius of Water—and the buildings that have surrounded it since it was dedicated almost 142 years ago. I have walked by the fountain almost every day for 25 years and knew a little about it. As part of writing this book, I learned a lot about it and also about its patron, Henry Probasco. I also learned a great deal about how interior United States cities were built beginning in the late eighteenth century, why they were built, why some cities succeeded and why other cities did not. I was pleasantly surprised to learn that the downtown street grid was laid out by Cincinnati's founders in early 1789 and that this grid remains substantially the same in 2013. I knew that Cincinnati was a large city in the 1850s and beyond, but I had no idea how big it had gotten within 62 years of its founding in 1788. Great fortunes were made and lost amid the explosive growth of what was the sixth-largest city in the United States. Probasco's fortune made from the hardware store business during the midst of the city's growth spurt is directly responsible for Cincinnati's fountain. This book also allowed me, with a little work, to incorporate a little of my passion for Civil War history. I learned that Abraham Lincoln in 1859 gave an important speech on the eastern side of the land surrounding what would become the square twelve years later. I also learned the story about Generals Grant and Sherman meeting in March 1864 in a parlor of the Burnet House, two blocks south of the land that would become the square, to lay the plans for the final campaigns of the Civil War that would end just over one year later.

David Ginsburg, the longtime president of Downtown Cincinnati Inc., was kind enough to contribute his thoughts about Fountain Square in his foreword to this book. I have been lucky to know David for the last sixteen years. We first met as neighbors, walking our dogs in Hyde Park. David introduced me to J. Miles Wolf, a longtime local photographer. Miles was kind enough to provide several pictures of the fountain and also of both the 1969 version of the square and the 2006 version.

As always, the folks at The History Press have been great to work with. Joe Gartrell, my commissioning editor, has been there with me every step along the way. Anne Shepherd and Linda Bailey at the Cincinnati Historical Society Library were helpful. The treasure-trove of material at the CHS Library is always fun to explore. Diane Mallstrom, Glen Horton and the people and resources at the downtown branch of the Public Library of Cincinnati and Hamilton County were wonderful. I have learned that our library is a much bigger resource than some of its critics appreciate. A visit to the Cincinnati Memory Project at www.cincinnatimemory.org is always worthwhile. Dan Prout furnished a number of images, each of which can be viewed at his website, www.cincinnativiews.net. My research assistants, Samantha Rogers and Brittany Doyle, are talented, lovely and hardworking. My law firm partners, Justin Flamm, Mark Stepaniak and Doreen Canton, again provided substantial assistance, as did my assistant, Sue Schmid.

The Taft Labor Department can feel a bit like an extended family at times. Two of my mentors, Roger A. Weber and J. Alan Lips, invested as much of their time in me as they could stand. They each influenced my life as much as any people I have known, and I thank them every day for their time and interest in me. They both left us far too young. I chose to dedicate this book to their memories. Thanks, Roger. Thanks, Alan.

No thank-you list would be complete without a shout out to my three children, Samantha, Parker and Caroline, and to my wonderful wife, Kathy. Thanks also to my aunt, Trish Smallenberger, for everything and especially for giving me the last bit of motivation that I needed to complete this project.

January 2013

INTRODUCTION

Fountain Square sits in what is now the center of downtown Cincinnati, and the fountain, whose theme is the Genius of Water and is known as the Tyler Davidson Fountain, sits in the middle of the square. While the current version of the square is the third one, over more than 140 years, the Genius of Water has remained the same. Since its 1871 dedication, it has long been Cincinnati's iconic figure.

Fountain Square is the living room of downtown Cincinnati. When an event happens, people congregate on the square. The World Choir Games took place, in part, on the square in the summer of 2012. Every time the Cincinnati Reds have won the World Series (five separate occasions spanning seventy-one years), the celebration happens there, as do many other kinds of celebrations. Political pep rallies occur there, as do protest marches. Kaiser Wilhelm I was burned in effigy there on Armistice Day, November 11, 1918. Wedding parties have their pictures taken on the square on Saturdays. Prom dates take their pictures there. Tourists take photographs. The situation comedy *WKRP in Cincinnati* filmed its opening sequence there.

In the winter, people ice skate on the square's large outdoor skating rink, which sits next to both an enormous decorated Christmas tree and also a large menorah that is illuminated during Hanukkah. Broomball matches take place in the rink on January and February weekday evenings. During the summer, events are held on the square's stage almost every weekday at lunchtime by one organization or another. Concerts of all types of music are held many nights. A lunchtime "wiener dog" race is held at the beginning

The nine-foot-tall Genius of Water has been the iconic image of Cincinnati since 1871. *Courtesy of J. Miles Wolf.*

This 2012 photograph shows the fountain and Fountain Square at lunchtime on a nice summer day. Downtown workers and many visitors routinely eat their lunches on the square. *Courtesy of J. Miles Wolf.*

of the city's Oktoberfest, the largest outside of Munich. German-style beer hall bands play on the square during the entire Oktoberfest weekend and are interrupted only for the world's largest "chicken dance." Downtown workers eat their lunches in the square on nice spring, summer and fall days.

The Tyler Davidson Fountain was dedicated on October 6, 1871, in a public ceremony attended by more than twenty thousand people, including Ohio governor and future president Rutherford B. Hayes. This image is from an engraving that was published by *Harper's Weekly* magazine one week earlier, on September 30, 1871. The engraving was made from a photograph of the fountain taken earlier in 1871 in Munich, home of the fountain's foundry. *From the library of Jim Tarbell.*

Why does Cincinnati have this fountain and Fountain Square? It is the brainchild of Henry Probasco, a hardware store merchant who became fabulously wealthy supplying the needs of Cincinnati residents in the 1850s when the population of Cincinnati grew by leaps and bounds. At that time, it was the nation's largest inland port, and it was among the ten largest cities in the country. Probasco retired in 1866 at the age of forty-six after the death of Tyler Davidson, his brother-in-law and business partner. It was long the dream of Davidson and Probasco to donate a monument to the city as their way of thanking their adopted hometown for its part in their success, and Probasco turned this dream into a reality.

The first square was a boulevard in the middle of Fifth Street from 1871 until the mid-1960s, when civic leaders recognized the need for urban renewal in the heart of the city. The second version of the square, located in the middle of a revitalized Fountain Square area complete with new buildings, was dedicated in 1969, and it lasted for thirty-six years. In the early 2000s, a new generation of civic leaders recognized the limitations of the 1969 design, and they came forward with a new design for the square that was dedicated in 2006. Through all three versions of the square, the fountain and the square have remained at the heart of downtown Cincinnati, integral to the image of the city.

The following chapters detail the beginning of the city of Cincinnati, explain why the square was placed where it was within the city's 1789 street grid, describe Probasco and his quest for this first American fountain of note and explain how the great Genius of Water came to be made. The book goes on to describe the buildings around the square since 1871, what happened to them and how and when the current buildings around the square came to be.

Chapter 1

Fountain Square Before the Square—Or the Fountain

Overview

Cincinnati was founded on December 28, 1788, by settlers looking to start a new community on land that was part of the Miami Purchase. The streets were laid out and the property platted by January 1789; much of this original street grid and plat design remains today, more than 220 years later. Native American claims on the land remained a source of friction with the white settlers. In late 1789, Fort Washington was built in Cincinnati to provide protection to the settlers. Through the 1795 Treaty of Greenville, the Indians agreed to vacate the southern part of the Ohio Territory, and Cincinnati grew rapidly. By 1850, Cincinnati was the sixth-largest city in the United States and the largest and most important city in the American West.

Third Street quickly became the preeminent thoroughfare in the city and the heart of the commercial district. The city's leading families lived in houses near today's Lytle Park, including the Longworth family, who owned the house that today is the Taft Museum.

In this era before electricity and refrigeration, the operation of public markets for butchers, fish sellers and produce vendors was a necessity in a city of any size. The Lower Market was founded in 1804 on Market Street, between Sycamore and Broadway and south of Third Street. Many more markets were founded over the years. Findlay Market was one such market, founded in 1852. Another such market, the Fifth Street Market founded in 1829, was demolished in 1870 to make room for Fountain Square.

The Miami Purchase

Perhaps the most abundant natural resource in America in the late eighteenth century was land, especially in the western territory outside the firm claims of any state. Immediately after the Revolutionary War, people were looking to get rich quickly by buying and selling land to those eager to leave the original thirteen states, move west, take advantage of the cheap farmland and make a new life. The new United States government had an interest in seeing the western lands become developed in order to fulfill its claims to the land, free from interference by Great Britain and France. A land syndicate led by John Cleves Symmes bought 311,682 acres from the federal government in southwestern Ohio on October 15, 1788, land known as the Miami Purchase. This purchase comprised all the land between the Little Miami River to the east and the Great Miami River to the west and was bordered on the north by a line near the northern borders of today's Butler and Warren Counties. The purchase took its name from the Miami Indians who inhabited this land at the time.

The Founding and Early Growth of Cincinnati, 1788–1819

The first settlers in the Miami Purchase landed at the confluence of the Little Miami and Ohio Rivers in November 1788, and they founded a town they named Columbia, which is today's Columbia Tusculum neighborhood. An obelisk sits in the middle of the Pioneer Cemetery, across Wilmer Avenue from the main terminal at Lunken Airport, which is in the vicinity of the spot where the landing occurred off the Little Miami River. (This bend in the Little Miami River was moved east in the early 1920s to make more room for the airport.) The first Nicholas Longworth (1783–1863) eventually came to own much of the land immediately north of the Columbia settlement, on which he planted vineyards to grow grapes to make wine. Longworth added the name Tusculum to the community. He borrowed this name from Tusculum, Italy, a town near Rome known for its wine.

Several months before the Columbia settlement was founded, on August 25, 1788, Matthias Denman (1760–1838), Robert Patterson (1753–1827) and John Filson (1747–88) entered into an agreement to found Cincinnati, and Denman put up the necessary cash to buy eight hundred acres from Symmes. Filson went on a surveying expedition near the Great Miami River, but he disappeared on October 1, 1788, when hostile Shawnees attacked his surveying party. His body was never found. Israel Ludlow (1765–1804), an accomplished surveyor, took Filson's place.

On December 28, 1788, this second group of settlers in the Miami Purchase landed at the confluence of the Licking and Ohio Rivers. On the north bank of the Ohio, they founded the town that Filson had called "Losantiville." This name was formed from the amalgamation of the Latin *os* (mouth), the Greek *anti* (opposite) and the French *ville* (city) from its position opposite and across from the mouth of the Licking.

Ludlow was tasked with laying out, distributing and selling lots within the town, and in January 1789, he devised the street grid system from Broadway (originally Eastern Row) to Central Avenue (originally Western Row) and from the river to Seventh Street, in a design copied from the street grid system of Philadelphia. Each square created by the cross streets was divided into eight lots, 99 by 198 feet, except for the land between Second and Third Streets and Water and Front Streets, which were smaller and larger, respectively, in order to accommodate changes made necessary by the hill rising from the river. Lots north of Seventh Street were sold in four-acre outlots (lots outside the town) for farming. The public square was placed at the southeastern corner of the town, and it became known as the public landing. A second square was dedicated between Fourth and Fifth Streets bounded by Main and Walnut as the original Government Square that was home to the first Hamilton County Courthouse. (Today the Mercantile Library Building is on this lot and Government Square has moved one block north.) Much of Ludlow's 1789 street grid north of Second Street remains in 2013.

The first thirty settlers in Cincinnati received for free both town and outlots on the conditions that they

> *became actual settlers on the premises; plant and attend two crops successively and* [that] *not less than One Acre shall be cultivated for each crop and that within the term of two years—each person...shall build a house equal to Twenty feet Square, One story and a half high with a brick*[,] *stone or clay Chimney which shall stand in front of their respective in lots and shall be put in tenable repair within the term of two years.*

The idea behind this grant of free land was that these settlers would found the town and make it attractive for others to land in Cincinnati and to buy their own lots.

The white settlers in the Miami Purchase ran into almost immediate problems with the Native Americans whom they were displacing against the will of the tribes, and a system of forts was created as a means to protect the newcomers. In Cincinnati, Major John Doughty arrived on August 16, 1789, and chose a site for a fort, named Fort Washington, on a commanding position overlooking the Ohio and Licking Rivers between Third and Fourth Streets and immediately east of Broadway. General Arthur St. Clair, a Revolutionary War veteran, was the first commander of Fort Washington, and he renamed the town "Cincinnati," after the Society of the Cincinnati, of which he was a member. This society was named for General George Washington, who like the Roman General Cincinnatus before him, returned to his farm after his days of leading his army campaign to a successful end instead of using his fame to become dictator over his country.

Hamilton County was formed on January 2, 1790, and Ludlow was named clerk. Ludlow later surveyed and laid out the street system in Hamilton, Ohio, in 1794. In 1795, with Governor Arthur St. Clair, Jonathan Dayton and William McMillan, Ludlow surveyed the town that later became Dayton, Ohio. In 1796, Ludlow built the largest house in Cincinnati, known as the Ludlow Mansion, which he lived in until his death in 1804.

In 1795, after they lost the Battle of Fallen Timbers, a number of Native American tribes signed the Treaty of Greenville, agreeing to leave the Miami Purchase and much of lower Ohio and lower Indiana. White settlers soon poured in as a result. Cincinnati was the largest settlement in the Miami Purchase, and it became large enough to be incorporated into a town in 1802, just fourteen years after its founding and one year before Ohio was admitted to the United States as the seventeenth state on March 1, 1803.

Fort Washington was abandoned by 1803, as it no longer was necessary once the Indians left, and the area around Lytle Park grew up near the site of the former fort with some of the town's nicest homes. In 1810, Cincinnati had 2,540 residents, making it the forty-sixth largest city in the country. The town grew so much that it was incorporated as a city in 1819, the same year Daniel Drake established the Medical College of Ohio there.

Continued Growth of Cincinnati, 1820–1870

Cincinnati grew from 9,642 residents in 1820, the fourteenth-largest city in the United States, to 216,239 residents by 1870, then the country's eighth-largest city. The city grew originally because of its strategic location on the Ohio River, which allowed relatively easy transportation of people, agricultural products and manufactured goods. Ludlow's decision to make one of the city's public squares the public landing was purposeful: it attracted both commerce and settlers. The Miami and Erie Canal opened from Cincinnati to Middletown by 1827, and it was then completed to Lake Erie by 1845, which further enhanced transportation. The canal came down the hill to the Ohio River on the route where Eggleston Avenue is today, from the current site of Central Parkway. It extended west and then north along the route of the parkway. The Cincinnati Subway later was built largely in the path of the canal, and Central Parkway thereafter was placed on top of this path. The subway construction took place from 1920 to 1925 when it was abandoned; it was never finished nor was it ever operational. The main subway tunnel runs under Central Parkway from Walnut Street to a spot north of the Western Hills Viaduct. Underground stations were built and still exist at Race Street, Liberty Street and Brighton's Corner.

Because of the city's location, farmers brought their livestock to the city to be slaughtered, and Cincinnati became a major meatpacking center, known by some as "Porkopolis." German immigrants especially flocked to the city beginning in the 1830s, and they centered immediately north of the Miami and Erie Canal in an area that derisively became known as Over-the-Rhine, i.e., the Germans lived "over the Rhine."

An early reference to the canal as "the Rhine" is from the 1855 book *White, Red, Black* in which Frederic Pulszky stated: "The Germans live all together across the Miami Canal, which is, therefore, here jocosely called the 'Rhine.'" The Irish also began to come in waves to the city in the 1840s, emigrating from Ireland due to the great potato famine. The year 1850 marked Cincinnati's highest relative population versus the rest of the country. With 115,435 residents, the city was the country's sixth largest.

The heart of the city and its financial district were centered along Third Street during this period, which sits on the first "shelf" that rises above the river. The Burnet House, at the northwest corner of Third and Vine Streets, was a prominent hotel during this time. It was there that Union army generals U.S. Grant and William Tecumseh Sherman, both Ohio natives,

The Burnet House, built in 1850, was a 340-room hotel located at the northwest corner of Third Street and Vine Street. Abraham Lincoln stayed here in September 1859 when he was campaigning for Republican candidates in Ohio, and he stayed here again on February 12, 1861, on his journey to Washington, D.C., to be sworn in as president. Generals U.S. Grant and William Tecumseh Sherman met here on March 20, 1864, to plan the Richmond and Atlanta campaigns that would end the Civil War the following spring. Other guests of note include Henry Clay, Daniel Webster, James Buchanan, Stephen A. Douglas, Salmon P. Chase and Horace Greeley. The hotel was razed in 1926. *Courtesy of the Public Library of Cincinnati and Hamilton County.*

met in Parlor A on March 20, 1864, to plan the Richmond and Atlanta campaigns that would end the Civil War about thirteen months later. It was not until the 1880s that Fourth Street, which sits on the second "shelf" north of the Ohio, started to became the preeminent business location.

The original well-to-do Cincinnatians settled in the eastern part of the city, along and around Lytle Square in the area formerly occupied by Fort Washington and the surrounding land on which the army officers had made their homes. One of these homes was built by prosperous local businessman Martin Baum in about 1820. It was later purchased by Nicholas Longworth in 1829 when Baum went bust. The home eventually was owned by Charles Phelps Taft (1843–1929), brother of President William Howard Taft (1857–1930). Charles Taft's wife, Anna Sinton Taft (1852–1931), was the daughter of David Sinton (1808–1900) and heiress to her father's immense pig iron fortune. David Sinton had bought the Baum house to live in, and he passed it on to his daughter and her husband, Charles, who determined to turn it into the Taft Museum of Art on the death of his wife.

The Public Markets, Including the Fifth Street Market

In this era before electricity and refrigeration, public markets were a necessity to sell perishable food to city residents. The Lower Market, later known as the Pearl Street Market, was built in 1804 on Market Street (which no longer exists), between Sycamore and Broadway Streets south of Third Street. The Sixth Street Market was started in 1826 and stretched

The Fifth Street Market was located in the middle of Fifth Street between Vine Street (which is shown) and Walnut Street on the far end. This image depicts the market and faces east toward Mount Adams. In 1870, when the market was razed to make room for Fountain Square, this part of downtown was disreputable (the financial district then was on Third Street). Local citizens wrote fountain patron Henry Probasco asking him to locate the fountain somewhere besides this part of Fifth Street, pointing out that the fountain would "be in the midst of Gambling halls, Grog shops and all kinds of characters[.]" *Courtesy of Cincinnati Museum Center–Cincinnati Historical Society Library.*

all the way from Central to Vine. The Fifth Street Market, site of today's Fountain Square, was built in 1829 on Fifth Street between Walnut and Vine on land deeded to the city "solely for construction of a market house." Another market built in 1829 was the Canal Market, located on Court Street between Vine and Walnut Streets. This market provided an outlet for foodstuffs traveling by barge on the Miami and Erie Canal, which was one block to the north. The Canal Market was torn down in 1864 to make room for the Court Street Market, which lasted until 1914. In 1848, the Wade Street Market was built between Wade and Bauer Avenues and was in business until 1898. Findlay Market, the only market that survives in 2013, was started in 1852 in the heart of Over-the-Rhine on Elder Street, between Elm and Race Streets. It was built on land donated by the estates of General James Findlay (1770–1835) and Jane Irwin Findlay (1769–1851). James Findlay moved to Cincinnati in 1793 and was Cincinnati's mayor in 1805 and 1810. He was also a general during the War of 1812. Findlay bought significant property north of Liberty Street in the area

Public markets, such as Findlay Market, were commonplace throughout early Cincinnati in the days before refrigeration and electricity. At one time there were markets on Pearl Street, Fifth Street, Sixth Street, Court Street and Wade Street. Findlay Market is the only market that survives. It was built on land given to the city by the estates of James and Jane Findlay for the express purpose of building a public market to be named for James Findlay, a United States general in the War of 1812. *Courtesy of J. Miles Wolf.*

known as the Northern Liberties. Part of this Northern Liberties property is the land on which Findlay Market sits today. Executors of the Findlay estate donated the land to the city, stipulating that it be used to build a public market named for General Findlay.

Fifth Street in 1870 was hardly the city center that it is today, for the financial and insurance companies found their homes at that time two blocks south along Third Street. The Fifth Street Market, with its fifty-four butchers, was considered an eyesore. No respectable woman would travel there unaccompanied by a man. It was a rough-and-tumble part of the city. Newspapers reported that the market was a disgusting site, denounced by the Board of Health.

Chapter 2

Henry Probasco and Tyler Davidson

The best-known landmark in Cincinnati has long been the Tyler Davidson Fountain, but of Tyler Davidson (1808–1865) little is known today. Davidson owned a hardware store downtown at 118 Main Street (currently about the site of Great American Ball Park), doing business as Tyler Davidson & Company. He hired Henry Probasco (1820–1902) as a clerk in 1835. Probasco became partners with Davidson in 1840, and in that same year, Probasco married Julia Carrington, Davidson's half sister. Thus Probasco became Davidson's brother-in-law as well as his business partner.

In 1851, Probasco persuaded Davidson that they should build their hardware store substantially larger than any then existing in Cincinnati, and it became a fabulous success. Sales tripled within three years, and Probasco and Davidson became wealthy in this era when Cincinnati's population grew by 600 percent, from 24,831 people in 1830 to 161,044 people in 1860.

Probasco spent eight months in Europe in 1856, and he was struck by the suburban residences of successful English merchants and manufacturers. On his return to Cincinnati, he was inspired to build his house, Oakwood, in the country, and he settled on the Clifton area for the construction of his Norman Romanesque Revival–style house. Clifton was not part of the city of Cincinnati at that time. It was incorporated as a village in 1850, and it was the neighborhood where many of those with means were settling, largely abandoning the Lytle Square area. (Clifton was not annexed by Cincinnati until 1896.) Probasco built Oakwood between 1859 and 1866 at a cost of $500,000. The home is an eleven-thousand-square-foot, sandstone and limestone structure designed by William Tinsley that originally was situated on an estate of twenty acres. A contemporary reviewer described the house:

> *On Lafayette avenue is situated the home and grounds of Henry Probasco, the gentleman who presented Cincinnati with the great fountain. They are the finest in the suburbs of Cincinnati. The grounds are spacious and varied in their attractions, and the house rich in all that delights the eye.*
>
> *The house is constructed of blue limestone. The quoins, angles and buttresses are of freestone, each piece of which is hammer-marked to make it harmonize with the rough limestone. The walls are of rubblework, the face of the stone having been untouched by chisel or hammer. The general*

Probasco built this house, which he called Oakwood, between 1859 and 1866 at a cost of $500,000. The house has eleven thousand square feet and was originally situated on twenty acres in the village of Clifton. Probasco was inspired to build this large suburban residence when he returned from an 1856 visit to England, where he became enchanted by the suburban residences of successful English merchants and manufacturers. *From Probasco's 1872 book,* The Tyler Davidson Fountain.

Oakwood was placed on the National Register of Historic Places on November 9, 1972. This photograph shows the home as it appeared in 2012. *Courtesy of the author.*

> *style is Anglo-Norman. It is one hundred and twenty feet long, fronting southwardly. In front is a massive stone terrace, which extends the entire length of the building. The house is entered through a magnificent stone porch, with elegant arches. At the northeast end of the edifice is a porte cochere, constructed of freestone, and the building is surmounted by a round tower, which springs from the walls of the main stairway. The whole external appearance of the building is one of spaciousness without useless room, of dignity without coldness, of variety without the loss of harmony…*
>
> *Deep ravines have been filled, elevations cut down and inequalities reconciled, until the present grounds bear no resemblance to their condition thirty-five years ago. Besides the beautiful lawns which surround Mr. Probasco's residence, he has almost every thing in the shape of shade and ornamental trees. In addition to the forest trees of America, he has a large collection of foreign beech, ash, oak, elm and maple, and a valuable collection of evergreens, gathered from various countries of the globe. The Pyrenees, the Himalayas and the Rocky Mountains have each made their contribution.*
>
> *Besides these, Mr. Probasco has a rosarium, in which he has four thousand roses. He has also a beautiful collection of variegated-leaf plants*

and hardy shrubs, together with many hardy ferns. This is a meager description of the floral beauties of this place. If space would permit, there could be given a formidable list of plants and flowers which the forests and gardens of the world have contributed. To complete the rare attractions of Mr. Probasco's place, he enjoys to the full extent the splendid panorama of the valley to the northward from his residence; thus combining in one home, the charming attractions of nature with the rich contributions of literature and art.

Henry Probasco was hired by Tyler Davidson at Davidson's hardware store in 1835. They became partners in 1840. Probasco persuaded Davidson to substantially enlarge the store in 1851 at the time when Cincinnati's population was booming. Probasco and Davidson made large fortunes selling hardware to the city's burgeoning population. The gift of the fountain was Probasco's way of thanking the city for his success. *Courtesy of Cincinnati Museum Center–Cincinnati Historical Society Library.*

The house, at 430 West Cliff Lane, was listed on the National Register of Historic Places on November 9, 1972. It remains well cared for on about one and a half acres of land that remain with the house.

Davidson and Probasco often discussed giving a monument to their adopted hometown to express their appreciation to the people of Cincinnati. They wanted this monument to be something both attractive and utilitarian. The business partners decided upon a gift of a fountain, but the Civil War delayed their plans. Davidson was in New York City in December 1865, when he died suddenly and was buried there.

After Davidson's death, Probasco sold his interest in Tyler Davidson & Company to Lowry, Perin & Company in March 1866, and he retired at the ripe old age of forty-five. Probasco then left for Europe, in part to find the fountain to give to the city of Cincinnati as he and Davidson had discussed. He found the fountain's design in Munich, Bavaria, in October 1866. (This was before the German unification that took place in 1871.) The making

This ten-foot-high fountain was donated by Probasco "to the people of Clifton in 1887," when Clifton was still a village, nine years before it was annexed by the city of Cincinnati. The fountain was designed by Samuel Hannaford, and it is built of bronze. It was added to the National Register of Historic Places in 1980. *Courtesy of the author.*

of the fountain and the terms of the gift to the people of Cincinnati would consume Probasco for the next five years.

During his European travels, Probasco assembled a first-rate collection of more than ten thousand books and rare manuscripts, which today are one of the foundations of the rare books collection of the Newberry Library in Chicago. He also developed an interest in horticulture, importing to his Oakwood estate trees and shrubs from all over the world. Probasco held important civic roles, including being a founder and president of Spring Grove Cemetery. He served on the village council of Clifton, and he later served as its mayor. He also was an original member of the Cincinnati Society for Natural History.

Probasco and his first wife, Julia, had no children, and she passed away in 1886. The year 1887 proved to be a very notable one for Probasco. That year, he married his second wife, Grace Sherlock, with whom he had two children: Grace, born in 1888, and Henry Jr., born in 1890. Probasco's son would pass away in 1901 at the age of ten, but his daughter Grace would go on to live a long life. She married John Jay Rowe, who would become one of the principals in what is known today as the Fifth Third Bank.

Also in 1887, Probasco would donate the Probasco Fountain to the Village of Clifton. The ten-foot-high fountain is located on Clifton Avenue near the intersection with Woolper Avenue. It was added to the National Register in 1980. It is built of bronze on a base of granite with an ornate design of chrysanthemums. It was designed by Samuel Hannaford, who also designed Cincinnati City Hall, Cincinnati Music Hall, the Cincinnati Observatory, Nast-Trinity Church, the Elsinore Arch and many other structures. Similar to the Genius of Water Fountain downtown, the Probasco Fountain in Clifton was built to be used as a drinking fountain. It has three different basins: a dipper once hung from the fountain for people, a larger basin was present for horses and a smaller basin was designed for use by dogs. This gift "to the people of Clifton" is inscribed: "Thirsty and ye gave me drink."

Unfortunately for Probasco, in 1887, he also suffered significant financial losses that caused him to have to sell his Oakwood mansion and move into a much smaller home. His fine collection of paintings and other artwork was auctioned to pay his creditors. Probasco was given a modest salary as superintendent of Spring Grove Cemetery, which he had earlier helped to found, and he was buried there on his death on October 26, 1902.

Chapter 3

Probasco Finds His Fountain Design in Munich

Overview

Probasco searched many European cities looking for a suitable design for what would become the Tyler Davidson Fountain. His challenge was to find a design that was both aesthetic and utilitarian but not chock-full of sea creatures, tritons, nymphs, gnomes or mythological creatures as was common at the time. Probasco found his design—a twenty-six-year-old creation for which no prior patron had been found—in Munich.

The original 1867 estimate to cast the fountain was $30,000, from Ferdinand von Miller, at the Royal Bavarian Foundries. Probasco somewhat increased the size of the fountain from the original quote, and it finally was finished at a cost of approximately $105,000. Miller originally promised delivery within three years, by 1870, but due to the increase in scope of the fountain and the travails wrought by the Franco-Prussian War, delivery was delayed by a year.

Meanwhile, back in Cincinnati, finding a site for the new fountain proved to be problematic. The city originally proposed Fifth Street between Walnut and Main Streets, but this plan fell through when the cost of relocating telegraph wires and streetcar rail lines proved to be too expensive. The new plan was to locate Fountain Square one block to the west, between Vine and Walnut Streets, to displace the ugly Fifth Street Market. The market's butchers fought their displacement all the way to the Ohio Supreme Court, ultimately without success.

The European Search

Probasco, his wife, Julia, and two female relatives left Cincinnati in 1866 for Europe, searching for a suitable design for the Cincinnati fountain. He reviewed many designs throughout Italy, Sicily and France and was disappointed to discover that most of these designs were based on mythological creatures, including Neptune, tritons and nymphs. Probasco and Davidson had talked about a fountain design that featured the blessings and utility of water. The historian Mary March notes that "Probasco also wanted the fountain to serve the purpose of keeping the young people of Cincinnati out of the coffee houses and provide an oasis of peace and cooling in the heart of the city."

The Probasco party eventually made its way to Munich into the Royal Bavarian Foundries of Ferdinand von Miller. (Bavaria was still an independent state at this time, a relic of the breakup of the Holy Roman Empire, and it would continue to be independent until the German unification in 1871.) King Ludwig I of Bavaria ("Mad King Ludwig") was the founder and patron of the foundries. Miller showed Probasco an 1840 drawing by Nuremburg painter and sculptor August von Krehling that was substantially the plan for the fountain for which Probasco had been searching. Miller had been hoping to find a patron to pay for the making of such a fountain, but his hopes had lasted fruitlessly some twenty-six years—the cost for the fountain exceeded even the purse of King Ludwig. Probasco asked Miller to make the fountain even more grand than the 1840 design, and he asked Miller to design the fountain to have a drinking fountain element as well. For this later purpose, Miller added the four small boys playing with a turtle, dolphin, goose and snake.

On February 15, 1867, Probasco wrote the Cincinnati City Council from Palermo, Sicily, offering to have the fountain and its base created and then to donate the fountain to the city. He stated:

> *Hon. Charles F. Wilstach, Mayor of Cincinnati:*
>
> *Dear Sir: I propose, in memory of the late Tyler Davidson, my brother-in-law, with whom, in his lifetime, I have frequently consulted, and who had the project much at heart, to erect a public fountain on the Fifth Street Market Space, near the intersection of Walnut street, to be made of Bavarian block granite, porphyry, and bronze, mainly according to the proposed design, of which a photograph is herewith presented.*
>
> *The entire height from the street to the top of the central figure (which will be seven feet high) will be thirty-two and a half feet. The estimated cost, in American gold, is thirty thousand dollars.*

The idea presented by this fountain is to represent the blessings and benefits of water. The principal figure represents the Genius of water, from whose hands fall the ever-flowing rain, the blessing of God, which is caught by a peasant on the right, whose fields are thirsting for it. On the opposite side stands a citizen imploring water for his burning house. The shell of the opposite side partly hides the figure of a young woman, who is offering water to her aged and decrepid [sic] *father. On the other side is a mother leading her child to the bath.*

Four bas-reliefs in the dies of the pedestal represent navigation, mills, fisheries, and steam.

On the corners of the pedestal are figures of children, suggesting the enjoyments connected with water, viz: a girl adorning herself with pearls; a boy fishing for shells; a second fitting on skates, and a third finding corals and crystals.

The portrait near the top of the entablature is designed to be a medallion of Tyler Davidson.

The water coming from the leaves of the shell is to be used as fresh drinking water by a separate conduit pipe, while the four upper jets only belong to the decoration.

The whole fountain will be of bronze, the base and its surroundings of granite and porphyry, the railings or protection of the foundation of wrought iron or Dayton stone.

The time required for the execution of this work in Munich is three years, and I hereby agree to place the fountain, complete, at the proposed spot on or before January 1, 1871, should the city accede to my wishes, so that I may have the information thereof in Paris by the middle of April.

All the expenses of every conceivable nature I propose to bear until the fountain is erected and in use, and accepted by the city, whose property it shall then become, subject to the following conditions:

1. The city shall maintain said fountain in complete order, and forever supply the drinking conduits with pure water for the free use of all who may resort thither at any hour of the day or night.

2 The ornamental conduits shall be fully supplied not less than twelve hours per day in June, July, August, and September; ten hours per day in April, May, October, and November, and six hours per day during the rest of the year, except when the thermometer is below the freezing point.

3. There shall be stationed at the fountain a proper and competent person, detailed from the police force or otherwise, employed and paid by the city, whose duty it shall be to keep it clean, and by day and night to guard it from injury, and protect all persons in the proper use thereof, as well as prevent any abuse of the same.

4. The water shall only be used for the drinking and ornamental purposes to which the fountain is devoted, except in case of fire.

I desire, also, to reserve the right of myself while living, or to my legal representatives, or any trustee whom I may appoint, or provide by deed or will for the appointment of, to hold the city responsible for the performance of these conditions, considering this as a gift to the people and a trust in the corporation.

I shall seek to make this fountain beautiful, and to have all its embellishments represent every-day life, each of which will be understood as soon as seen. I shall seem to make it beautiful in its form and practical in its uses. I shall use the everlasting bronze and granite, sparing nothing in care or money that the foundation and pipes and working parts shall be able to endure for at least a generation without repairs.

I must reserve the right, while not varying from this plan in any substantial respect, of making such changes in detail as may appear during the progress of preparation of the detailed drawings and clay models to enhance the beauty or utility of the design.

Will you do me the favor to lay my wishes before the council of your city? And, in the hope that the proposition I make may receive favorable consideration at their and your hands,

I am, very respectfully, yours, etc.,
Henry Probasco.

The City Council, on March 15, 1867, unanimously agreed to accept the gift under the conditions Probasco had asked. The city first pledged to construct an esplanade on Fifth Street between Walnut and Main Streets. The problem with this site was that the cost to relocate telegraph lines and streetcar lines would be cost prohibitive. It was redetermined to be placed on Fifth between Vine and Walnut, which was the site of the Fifth Street Market, considered by many to be an eyesore.

Probasco placed the order for the fountain with Miller on May 15, 1867. The original plan for the fountain had the main Genius of Water figure at six feet and the height of the entire fountain twenty-nine and a half feet. Over time, the plans changed so that the height of the main figure became nine feet and the total height of the fountain became thirty-eight feet.

Krehling was called upon to sculpt the central figure, the Genius of Water, and the four principal figures surrounding it. He also was selected to sculpt the four bas-reliefs depicting the various uses of water. Miller's son Ferdinand was assigned the task of sculpting the four drinking fountains, including the affectionately nicknamed "Turtle Joe." Miller suggested to Probasco that he send photographs of Davidson and him so that Miller could cast medallions of their likenesses to affix to the top of the fountain. But the ever-humble Probasco chose instead the inscriptions, "To the People of Cincinnati, Henry Probasco–Tyler Davidson, MDCCCLXXI."

The granite and marble were mined from the mountains of Saxony. Miller made many trips there to inspect the stone. He wrote to Probasco both to describe the beauty of the stone but also to assure Probasco that the stone was impervious to being cracked by cold weather.

Probasco had projected that the fountain would be in Cincinnati by January 1, 1871, and that it would cost him $30,000. By the time it was complete, the project cost Probasco in excess of $100,000, and it was delivered almost one year late. Significant correspondence describes ongoing agitation on both sides between Probasco and Miller. Probasco, of course, had greatly enlarged the fountain from its original size. The Franco-Prussian War caused part of the delay as well. Miller's sons and workmen all fought in the war, and one of his workmen lost a leg in battle. Miller referred Probasco to the travails wrought by the recently ended American Civil War in trying to point out the logistical burdens the war was having on completion of the fountain.

The fountain finally was completed in the summer of 1870, and in Munich it was assembled and tested. The next concern became whether to ship the fountain to America by steamer or sailing ship. Shipment by sail would be half the cost of shipment by steamer, but it also would be more expensive to insure and would delay delivery considerably. Probasco finally decided to ship by steamer. The sixty crates containing the fountain were shipped north on ten railroad cars to Hamburg, where they would be loaded onto the steamers. Miller had to enlist a German minister of trade to secure these railroad cars at a time when German trains were still shipping home French prisoners of war at the conclusion of the Franco-Prussian War. Transportation was especially difficult given that the semicircular pieces composing the base each weighed eighteen thousand pounds.

The steamers finally made it to New York City, from where Miller's son Ferdinand and a workman from the foundry traveled with the pieces of the fountain to Cincinnati by train. Young Ferdinand von Miller stayed seventy-eight days in the city, lodging at the Burnet House, to oversee the installation of the fountain. The relationship between the senior Miller and Probasco had reached its ebb at this point. Probasco was exasperated by the costs involved, which were significantly higher than he had been quoted. Miller thought that Probasco had significantly enlarged the design from the original quotation and, further, that he failed to understand the financial realities of bringing such a large project to fruition.

The Fifth Street Market Controversy

The setting of Fountain Square—which originally was called Probasco Place or the Probasco Esplanade—caused quite a furor. Some people thought that the Fifth Street location was simply a poor idea. On February 18, 1869, J.W. McLaughlin wrote to Probasco and suggested a location near Eighth and Race Streets for the site, noting the potential problem of the restrictive covenants on the Fifth Street Market space that required that the land be used for a public market. Joseph S. Hill wrote to Probasco a lengthy letter on July 22, 1869, part of which urges Probasco to find

> *a more agreeable place than 5th Street where it will be in the midst of Gambling halls, Grog shops and all kinds of characters, which are now around it* [Fifth Street]. *Strangers visiting the City and the Fountain would far prefer seeing it on the Park than in the centre of what is 5th and Vine or Walnut is... Ask Mrs. Probasco if she would like to walk up from 4th either Walnut, Vine or Race Street unattended by a Gentleman to view the same. If I have intruded on you, you will please excuse me, as I do not wish to be obtrusive. The removal of the Market House or shed on 5th I am in favour of.*

The Fifth Street Market with its fifty-four butchers was unquestionably an eyesore, but half of the property was deeded to the city with covenants restricting use of the land to be used for a public market. One of these covenants stated that the conveyance was "for the sole use and purpose of erecting a market-house and for a market space, and for no other use and purpose whatever." The butchers sued to prohibit the demolition of the market and the erection of Fountain Square on the site of the Fifth Street Market in a case that was ultimately decided by the Ohio Supreme Court on February 1, 1870.

The court noted that "the present market house is a very old and unsightly edifice, which has been declared a public nuisance by the board of health of the city." The court's opinion goes on to state:

> *The city has accepted an offer from Henry Probasco to erect, at his expense, on the ground now covered by the eastern half of the market house, a free public drinking fountain, which, it is averred, will be an ornament to the city, a work of art of great and lasting benefit to the owners of the adjacent lots, and a convenience to those who may frequent that part of the city for market or other purposes, and which, it is said, is a proper and frequent addition to market spaces, and not inconsistent with the use of the ground for such purpose.*

The Supreme Court found that "on the continent of Europe, fountains of the character of the one proposed are frequently found in the public market places." It stated that the destruction of the market and the erection of the fountain and esplanade were not inconsistent with the restrictive covenants requiring a market place be present on the land, and it allowed the construction of the square and the destruction of the market.

The City Council took no chances that the butchers would interfere with the destruction of the market. The police, street cleaners and ninety city workers carrying axes, crowbars and ladders were told to stand at the ready at 3:00 p.m. on Friday, February 4, 1870, when the City Council voted, twenty-five to eight, to have the market razed. Minutes later the city workers were told to get to work, and by 6:00 p.m. that afternoon, the market was gone. The butchers later were paid $500 apiece in compensation, which added some $27,000 to the city's cost for the fountain. Out of an abundance of caution over the restrictive covenant, once a year, flowers were sold on Fountain Square in order to fulfill the covenant that the land be used as a marketplace. This problem finally was solved forever in the 1960s when the city successfully filed an action to quiet its title to the property.

Chapter 4

The October 6, 1871 Dedication of the Fountain

The fountain was dedicated in a large public ceremony on Friday, October 6, 1871, beginning at eleven o'clock. Rows of temporary benches were erected on the north and south sides of the square to accommodate four thousand guests. Estimates of the total crowd over the course of that day range from a minimum of twenty thousand to a maximum of fifty thousand.

The speakers and dignitaries assembled at the Burnet House two blocks south of the square, and they departed at a quarter to eleven to arrive at the designated time. Archbishop John B. Purcell gave the invocation that day. Purcell noted:

> *The history of pagan and Christian Rome commemorates the imperial and pontifical achievements which conveyed from distant mountains the waters that refreshed the million dwellers in the Eternal City, and that bound to-day in undiminished volume from the fountains of the Vatican and Trevi. These glorious works, and those of the grand monarch at Versailles, we of the Queen City need not envy. As long as grass grows and water runs, we shall enjoy the healthful, cooling draughts of the Tyler Davidson fountain. These draughts we can drink in conscious security that, unlike those of certain other cities, they contain no impure admixture of animal, mineral, or vegetable matter. For we can assure our friends from abroad that, whatever may be said of the Ohio, as was said of the yellow Tiber, we have found the secret of presenting it as pure, as crystalline to the lip, as ever flowed from nature's secret springs, or were distilled from chemical alembic.*

This print shows the fountain and Fountain Square in 1872, when it was originally placed in a park on Fifth Street between Vine Street and Walnut Street. The fountain is shown considerably large and out of scale. The buildings around the square would change relatively quickly. Mabley & Carew would build its first store in 1881 on the northeast corner of Fifth and Vine where the Fountain Clothing Store is depicted in this image. The print describes Fountain Square as "Probasco Place." The name did not stick. *From the library of Jim Tarbell.*

Ohio governor (and later president) Rutherford B. Hayes spoke. His speech noted that Cincinnati in 1871 was the center of midwestern life, and he also emphasized the theme later trumpeted by Andrew Carnegie about the "Obligation of Wealth." Governor Hayes stated:

> *But this fountain does not pour out its blessings for Cincinnati, or for her visitors and guests, alone. Cincinnati is one of the central cities of the nation, and of the great continent. It is becoming the convention city. Witness the national assemblies in the interest of commerce, of industry, of education, of benevolence, of progress, of religion, which annually gather here from the most distant parts of America. This monument is an instructor of all who come. Whoever beholds it will carry away some part of the lesson it teaches. The duty which the citizen owes to the community in which and by which he has prospered—that duty this work will forever teach. No rich man, who is wise, will, in the presence of this example, willingly go to his grave with his debt to the public unpaid and*

unprovoked for. Many a last will and testament will have a beneficent codicil, suggested by the work we inaugurate to-day. Parks, fountains, schools, galleries of art, libraries, hospitals, churches, whatever benefits and elevates mankind, will here receive much needed encouragement and support.

Next, prominent local attorney William Groesbeck spoke. Groesbeck was a pro-Union Democrat during the Civil War and served in the United States House of Representatives. Groesbeck came to national prominence as a key member of the legal team in 1868 that successfully averted the conviction of President Andrew Johnson by the U.S. Senate of the articles of impeachment that had been passed by the House of Representatives. Groesbeck returned home to Cincinnati and later built his beautiful estate, Elmhurst, in the new neighborhood of Hyde Park. Groesbeck talked of the artistic merit of the fountain:

I have said, my friends, that this is a rare gift, an uncommon gift, a gift of a kind not often made. Fountains of high artistic design, and sculptural decorations, were common enough in ancient times. We are told that in Greece every principal city had one, and many of them were celebrated for their elegance and beauty. And this ancient custom has survived to some extent, for they still abound in Rome. Paris is famous for them; but we very seldom see them in modern cities, and I know of no other than this in our country worthy of particular mention.

Dr. Max Lilienthal, rabbi of the Jewish synagogue on Mound Street, next was called upon to speak. Lilienthal was born in Munich, and he emphasized the connections between the Queen City of the West and his former home across the sea. Then young Ferdinand von Miller, son of the fountain's designer, was introduced, and he gave a short speech about the thanks that his family had for Probasco's munificence.

Henry Probasco was the next speaker, and as was his right, he spoke at great length. He spoke of his wish for those who would use the fountain. He stated:

Standing here in this growing city of the West, this fountain, by day and by night, will pour forth its gladdening waters from the hands of the genius above, whose serene countenance, radiant with love, faces the east, the place of paradise, the source of light, dispensing her benison in the name of its founder, for generations to come. Its streams will strengthen many a Samson for fresh conflict with the Philistines of intemperance and lust, and, like

Probasco published a book in 1872 to commemorate the dedication of the fountain the year before. This photo is from Probasco's book. The Genius of Water faces east, toward Mount Adams and Munich, where she was cast at the Royal Bavarian Foundries. This version of Fountain Square lasted from 1871 until 1966. *From Probasco's 1872 book,* The Tyler Davidson Fountain.

> *an angel, give hope and life to the Hagars and Ishmaels in the dreary wilderness of their sojournings. Here at the moving of the waters, will descend the presiding angel of health and healing, and send the processions of pilgrims, who shall gather here, rejoicing on their way.*

Probasco concluded with the powerful idea behind the fountain, that of Davidson and Probasco wishing to thank their adopted hometown for their mighty financial successes by returning to the city a portion of that success:

> *There is no doubt the city of Cincinnati will preserve it in grateful recollection her two sons, who, at the end of a long business career as merchants remembered with filial devotion the city of their adoption; that she will throw around it every protection and support needful to perpetuate it as a trust for the people, and that her citizens will value it for its worth and meaning, and cherish it as an example of philanthropic munificence.*

Cincinnati mayor S.S. Davis then was called upon to accept the Tyler Davidson Fountain on behalf of the city. Davis stated:

> *I thank you, sir, not so much for the expenditure of your means, for that I know you make with pleasure, as for the donation of your valuable time, and the giving of your excellent taste and judgment to the formation of this great and useful object. Money alone—though it might have secured a space, an esplanade, a foundation and a fountain—could not have secured your taste and judgment.*

As Davis was making his remarks, young Ferdinand von Miller took the tarp off the Genius of Water, and it was unveiled to the assembled crowd. The brand-new Fountain Square was mobbed until midnight with townspeople vying to get a glimpse of the fountain. The United States Army band from the barracks at Newport, Kentucky, provided music until ten o'clock that evening. Calcium lights were trained upon the fountain for illumination.

The following day the *Cincinnati Commercial* newspaper remarked on the transformative effect the new fountain was having on the neighborhood and the city itself. It stated that "when, as a radiant educator in our midst, it has transformed the dingy blocks about it, creating in the surroundings a fitness with itself, its reputation, as well for loveliness as for appositeness, far extended and acknowledged, will be a recognized part of the wealth of the city; and it will be, perhaps not one of the wonders, but certainly one of the graces of the world."

Chapter 5

The Tyler Davidson Fountain

Overview

The Tyler Davidson Fountain is the earliest fountain of note in the United States. The fountain's theme is the Genius of Water. Henry Probasco searched far and wide for a fountain depicting the utility and blessings of water, and in August von Krehling's 1840 design he found it. The four small figures of boys with a turtle, a snake, a goose and a fish were not part of the original Krehling design. Probasco wanted his fountain to be beautiful, but he also wanted it to be utilitarian—it is an enormous drinking fountain, and the four boys are the drinking part of the fountain. Cups were cast in Munich and attached by chains to the statues of the boys for Cincinnatians to claim a drink of water from the ice-cooled reservoir sitting under the base of the fountain. Probasco had the fountain constructed as a gift to his adopted hometown and also to honor his brother-in-law, Tyler Davidson.

Measurements

The bronze fountain is thirty-eight feet high, and it weighs twenty-four tons. The entire statue, including the base, stands at forty-three feet. The central figure is nine feet high and weighs two tons. The circular basin and

These four photographs from 1872 demonstrate all four sides of the Tyler Davidson Fountain, which was designed to illustrate the Genius of Water and the bounty that it provides. The photographs also show the short and relatively quaint buildings around the square at that time. *From Probasco's 1872 book,* The Tyler Davidson Fountain.

base of the fountain is made of porphyry—a purple-red form of igneous rock—quarried in Bavaria, and it weighs eighty-five tons. It cost Probasco about $110,000 to have it constructed and shipped. It is estimated that five hundred gallons of water flow through the fountain every minute.

The Genius of Water

The nine-foot-high Genius of Water is the central figure of the statue. She stands in flowing robes with outstretched arms and water falling from the 438 holes in each hand onto the four shaft figures surrounding her. Her pedestal has four inscriptions. Directly under her toes is the inscription, "To the People of Cincinnati." Behind her is inscribed the year of the fountain's dedication, "MDCCCLXXI," or 1871. "Tyler Davidson" is inscribed on the pedestal under her left arm, and "Henry Probasco" is inscribed on the pedestal under her right arm. The fountain is cast out of bronze, made out of cannons that were purchased from the Dutch government and melted down.

The Shaft Groups

The fountain has four shaft groups that illustrate the blessings of water. Each sculpture is about seven feet high. The group on the side under the face of the Genius of Water is a partially nude mother directing her naked and obviously reluctant boy to the bath. The group behind the Genius is an old man on crutches, holding a glass of water that his daughter, who is holding a pitcher, has supplied to him. The face of the daughter is a likeness of Krehling's daughter. To the Genius's right hand is a farmer, imploring rain to fall on his fields, with his dog in obvious distress and in need of water. To the Genius's left hand is a man with an empty bucket, looking to the heavens to fill it so that he may fight the fire on the roof of a structure from which flames are erupting. The farmer and the would-be firefighter are placed under the hands of the Genius so that they continuously receive the blessings of water.

The four shaft groups, each about seven feet high, illustrate the blessings of water. The group on the top left shows a mother taking her reluctant son to the bath. The group on the top right is a farmer hoping for rain to fall on his fields. The bottom left group shows a man seeking rainwater to fill his bucket to help fight a fire. The bottom right group shows a daughter helping her invalid father with a glass of water. *From Probasco's 1872 book,* The Tyler Davidson Fountain.

The Bas-Relief

The four bas-relief plaques on the pedestal under the Genius depict the uses of water. The bas-relief on the front of the fountain shows fishermen with their full nets, struggling to land their catch. The plaque behind the Genius shows water powering a water wheel that is milling corn brought by

This bas-relief was on the south side of the fountain in 1871; as of 2013, it is on the west, the fountain having been moved twice in the intervening years. This sculpture shows a steamboat sailing away, to represent navigation. *From Probasco's 1872 book,* The Tyler Davidson Fountain.

This bas-relief is on the fountain's east side in 2013. It shows workmen shaping bars of iron under a hammer powered by a steam engine. *From Probasco's 1872 book,* The Tyler Davidson Fountain.

In 1871, this bas-relief was on the west; in 2013 it is on the north side of the fountain. It demonstrates a water wheel milling corn brought by peasants. *From Probasco's 1872 book,* The Tyler Davidson Fountain.

This bas-relief is directly under the toes of the Genius of Water, and it demonstrates fishermen with full nets, struggling to bring in their catch. *From Probasco's 1872 book,* The Tyler Davidson Fountain.

peasants. The bas-relief to the fountain's left hand shows workmen shaping bars of iron under a hammer powered by a steam engine. The plaque to the Genius's right shows a steam ship sailing away from a party left at shore to represent navigation.

Next page: These four niche figures adorn the four corners of the fountain. On the top left, a boy has pulled a lobster from his net. The top right shows a girl holding a shell to her ear to listen to the crash of ocean waves. The bottom left shows a boy putting on his ice skates. And the bottom right shows a girl dressed in pearls and staring at her reflection in the water. *From Probasco's 1872 book,* The Tyler Davidson Fountain.

The Four Niche Figures

There is a figure in each of the four niches surrounding the pedestal. The first is of a semi-naked boy who has pulled a lobster from his fishing net. The second is a young boy sitting while putting on his ice skates. The third figure is of a girl dressed in pearls and staring at her reflection in the water. The fourth is of a girl holding a shell up to her ear, listening to the crash of the ocean waves.

The four drinking fountains were not part of the original 1840 design by Nuremburg sculptor August von Krehling. Probasco added them to the design to make the fountain utilitarian as well as beautiful. The design as finished is an enormous drinking fountai The original 1871 design for the chambers under the fountain contained room for quantities of ice to cool the drinking water during the summer months. Rafted which the public could drink, were chained to each of the four boys. The four depicted with an animal—one with a turtle, another with a dolphin, a third and the fourth with a goose. *From Probasco's 1872 book,* The Tyler Davidso

The Drinking Fountains

Krehling's original design for the fountain did not have drinking fountains, but Probasco wanted his fountain to be both artistic and utilitarian, so he commissioned Miller to add drinking fountains to the design. The four boys that are far to the fountain's exterior are those drinking fountains, though they have not been used for this purpose for quite some time. Cups were commissioned and attached by chains to the fountain so that visitors to the Genius could enjoy a cool glass of water. The lack of proper hygiene obvious with this design caused it to be discontinued.

Each of the four boys is naked and is depicted interacting with a different animal. Water is dispensed from the lips of the animals. One figure, "Turtle Joe," is so named because he rides the back of a large turtle. Another attempts to crush the head of a snake that has coiled itself around his foot. A third figure is riding a dolphin, and the fourth has caught and is playing with a goose.

Pipes and Chambers

In 1871, the drinking fountains and the two jets of the lower fountain were supplied by the regular city reservoir, but this water source generated insufficient pressure to fuel the hands of the Genius. Her fountains were connected, instead, by pipe to the Mount Auburn Reservoir, 350 feet above the fountain. The drinking fountains were designed to dispense ice water, and for this purpose a chamber twelve feet deep by ten feet square was constructed under the fountain and filled with ice. Two thousand feet of pipe covered the room, going through the ice to chill the water as it made its way to the drinking fountains.

The Base and Basin

h weight of the superstructure, when the basin is filled, is about two su ed tons, and so the support for the base and basin is necessarily Th ial. The exterior of the circular basin is forty-three feet around. f the basin, at twenty inches, is dark, polished porphyry that was

This photograph was taken sometime between 1889, when the Carew Building (left) was built by Joseph Carew, and 1929, when it was demolished. The Mabley & Carew Department Store building (right) was finished in 1881, and it remained on the square until the redevelopment of the late 1960s. *Courtesy of the Public Library of Cincinnati and Hamilton County.*

quarried in the Fichtel Mountains of Bavaria. The pedestals of the four drinking fountains are made from the same material.

The base on which the fountain stands is a quatrefoil in form and is made up of eight blocks of the same Bavarian porphyry, weighing forty tons. When the fountain is going, about half of the highly polished base is submerged.

Original Use of the Fountain

A study was done on August 10 and 11, 1872, to determine the fountain's usage from 6:00 a.m. on the tenth until 6:00 a.m. on the eleventh. In this twenty-four-hour period, 117 buckets and pitchers were filled with ice water. Persons drinking from the fountain were counted as follows:

Hours	No. of People	Hours	No. of People
6 to 7 a.m.	400	6 to 7 p.m.	214
7 to 8	371	7 to 8	593
8 to 9	324	8 to 9	827
9 to 10	356	9 to 10	763
10 to 11	389	10 to 11	660
11 to 12	392	11 to 12	133
12 to 1 p.m.	313	12 to 1 a.m.	58
1 to 2	350	1 to 2	26
2 to 3	217	2 to 3	22
3 to 4	111	3 to 4	20
4 to 5	269	4 to 5	31
5 to 6	273	5 to 6	90

Chapter 6

Fountain Square, Version 1

The Fountain Faces East, 1871–1969

The original Fountain Square was created as a boulevard in the middle of Fifth Street between Vine and Walnut Streets. Henry Probasco's deal with the city was that he would pay for the fountain and the city would pay for the esplanade. The first version of the square was elliptical at four hundred feet long by sixty feet wide, and it was constructed for $75,000. It was designed by the architect William Tinsley, who earlier had drawn up the plans for Probasco's home, Oakwood, in Clifton. The city paid for sixteen lampposts around the esplanade's borders, as well as the underground ice chamber to cool the drinking water provided by the fountain. The face of the Genius of Water pointed east, toward Mount Adams and ultimately toward Munich, where she was made. The city named the square Probasco Place, but the name did not take. The name Fountain Square was used from the beginning.

The fountain, which cost Probasco about $110,000 to have built, was not cheap for the city to operate. City records from 1872 reflect the total cost of operations for the fountain that year as the astronomical sum of $10,000, which included the cost of ice and the wage of $2.00 per day for the day watchman and $2.50 per day for the night watchman.

Also in 1872, less than a year after the fountain was dedicated, some enterprising soul determined he could improve upon Miller's sculpture of the Genius's hands—and the 438 holes in each—and destroyed the functionality of the hands in the process. Miller graciously agreed to make replacements and send them to Cincinnati on completion.

Probasco grew unhappy with the manner in which the city maintained the fountain and the square. In 1894, Probasco wrote the city a letter complaining

This view, looking east, shows the 1881 Mabley & Carew Department Store building on the left and the second version of the Gibson Hotel on the right, built in 1873 just after the 1871 dedication of Fountain Square. Produce stands in the foreground are waiting on customers. *Courtesy of Cincinnati Museum Center–Cincinnati Historical Society Library.*

about the lack of maintenance of the fountain, about the decision to replace the original oak benches with less elegant benches and about the decision to discontinue employment of the day and night watchmen, which the city had agreed to do in perpetuity when Probasco agreed to pay for the construction of the fountain. In time, the city stopped providing ice for chilled water, too, as a means to cut costs. It was not until 1902, thirty-one years after the fountain's dedication, that it was cleaned for the first time.

In 1870, the city won the fight with the butchers over the restrictive covenants concerning the land under half of the square requiring the perpetual use of the land for markets. The city won by arguing that the presence of a fountain was not inconsistent with the use of the land as a market. The conditional use as a market was complied with by having the mayor buy one flower there each year so that the city could argue that it continued to use the land as a marketplace. It was not until the

This drawing faces toward the east. The 1923 version of the Gibson Hotel is shown at right with the flag flying from its roof, near the Albee Theater. The United States Post Office and Courthouse, shown on the upper left, was in service from 1885 until 1936. *Courtesy of the Public Library of Cincinnati and Hamilton County.*

1960s that the city sued to quiet the title and eliminate the restrictions on the use of the land.

When the design for Fountain Square was made in 1871, there were no automobiles. The square's effect on traffic congestion with the advent of the car was less than optimal. By 1930, with the automobile commonplace, traffic congestion around the fountain had grown so bad that the city manager proposed moving it to the new Union Terminal that was then under construction. The *Commercial Tribune* reported on March 16, 1930, that "as arranged at present nearly all congestion originates in the Fountain Square area." Public outrage at the proposal quickly quashed it. Many newspaper stories quoted city residents who noted that Fountain Square was the city's "living room" and that it would be a mistake to move the city's signature artistic piece away from the heart of downtown. F. Mills Judy, vice-president of the Myers Y. Cooper Company, spoke for many when he stated:

> *The fountain is as much an institution of Cincinnati as the Ohio River. A city must have some tradition. Practically all the larger cities of the country have some square in their downtown section. In Detroit there is Cadillac square; Cleveland has its Soldiers and Sailors' monument in the heart of its*

Paul Briol was a well-known Cincinnati photographer, and he took this iconic photograph sometime after the RKO Albee opened in 1927. This photo shows the fountain's original orientation, which faced to the east. *Courtesy of Cincinnati Museum Center–Cincinnati Historical Society Library.*

> *downtown section. Should the fountain be removed the square would appear drab and colorless and have the dreary appearance of Government square. The fountain and the esplanade should be preserved.*

The fountain has undergone a number of changes over the years. In 1932, electric floodlights were installed to illuminate the fountain at night. These lights were turned off in December 1941 for the duration of World War II. They were turned on again in 1946 and have remained on since. A water-display pipe ring was added to the fountain's basin in 1949, creating 240 thin jets of water. This ring remained in use until the fountain's restoration in the year 2000.

Chapter 7

Fountain Square, Version 2

The Fountain Faces West, 1969–2005

The 1871 original design for Fountain Square itself was a rather modest boulevard where the park containing the fountain was a four-hundred-foot by sixty-foot island in the middle of Fifth Street. This design predated the invention of the automobile. Traffic congestion caused by the design made pedestrian traffic to the square difficult. The relatively small size of the square made it impossible to hold large events there.

The 1964 "Plan for Downtown Cincinnati" called for a new Fountain Square, to be made into a spacious pedestrian plaza over the top of the northern part of the Fifth Street Boulevard, anchored on Vine Street. The fountain would be moved to the southwest corner of the plaza and turned to face west, visible down Fifth Street to car traffic headed east. The plan also called for the demolition of the old retail buildings on the north side of Fifth Street, the demolition of the sixteen-story office tower at the corner of Fifth and Walnut Streets and the construction of a new, taller office building in its place. This plan called for a completely new reconstruction of the central part of the city.

RTKL, a Maryland architecture and urban planning firm, was hired to create a new parking garage under the new Fountain Square. The garage was planned to attract people back into downtown. The Maryland firm also was hired to design the new Fountain Square. In the new urban plan, Fountain Square was designated "Block A" as it was the key block to the revitalization of downtown. A Working Review Committee designated by the city was put in place to shepherd the project along. This committee was headed by Mark Upson, a retired Procter & Gamble executive.

Construction on the new four-level parking garage designed with space to park 615 vehicles was started on January 10, 1966, and the garage opened

Fountain Square was redone and rededicated in 1969. The fountain was turned 180 degrees and placed on the square's southwest corner, facing drivers coming east on Fifth Street. This photograph shows the square as it appeared shortly before it was redone sometime shortly before 2000, when the fountain itself was revitalized. As part of this renovation, the ring of jets in the base that was installed in 1949, shown propelling the 240 thin jets of water, was removed to restore the fountain to its original 1871 appearance. *Courtesy of J. Miles Wolf.*

on April 22, 1967. The city charged fifteen cents per half hour to park, up to a maximum of $3 a day. Parking revenue was devoted to paying off the construction costs of $2,958,000.

Work on the new Fountain Square began on December 11, 1967, and the new square was rededicated on October 18, 1969, ninety-eight years and twelve days after the original dedication. The fountain was placed off-center on the new square, close to the corner of Fifth and Vine Streets. The Genius of Water was turned 180 degrees to face due west, readily visible to car traffic headed east on Fifth Street. The work just to redo the square was $2,035,000. Cincinnati mayor Eugene P. Ruehlmann was the master of ceremonies at the dedication celebration, and speakers included Dr. Emerson Colaw, pastor of the Hyde Park Community United Methodist Church; James A. Rhodes, Ohio governor; Fred Lazarus III, president of the Greater Cincinnati Chamber of Commerce; and Francis L. Dale, who

The 1964 "Plan for Downtown Cincinnati" called for the redevelopment of large parts of downtown, including especially Fountain Square. Construction began in January 1966. This photograph shows the entire block having already been demolished later that year with the exception of the sixteen-story Fountain Square Building, which had retail on the first floor and offices above. The fountain is visible on the lower right, cased in scaffolding. *Courtesy of Cincinnati Museum Center–Cincinnati Historical Society Library.*

This May 1968 photograph shows Fountain Square under reconstruction. The DuBois Tower, to the upper center, is about halfway complete. The Fifth Third parking garage and executive offices are partially finished near the site of the former Mabley & Carew Department Store. The Sheraton Gibson Hotel and the RKO Albee Theater are visible at the bottom right. *Courtesy of Cincinnati Museum Center–Cincinnati Historical Society Library.*

was both publisher of the *Cincinnati Enquirer* and chairman of the Fountain Square Functions Committee. Erich Kunzel led the Cincinnati Symphony Orchestra in the prelude.

Part of the Fountain Square renovation included the demolition of all the buildings on the north side of Fifth Street and a plan to put up new office towers on part of the square. Before the renovation, lining the block on the north were the 1881 Mabley & Carew Building on the northwest corner of Fifth and Vine Streets, several smaller retail offices and theater buildings along Fifth Street toward Walnut Street and the sixteen-story Fountain Square office building on the northeast corner of Fifth and Walnut Streets.

All these buildings were demolished, and the new office buildings built in their place were finished in 1969. Fifth Third Union Trust Company was convinced to commit to the $20 million construction project that built a thirty-two-story building at the corner of Fifth and Walnut Streets and a

The thirty-two-story Fifth Third Bank Tower dominates the eastern edge of Fountain Square. *Courtesy of the author.*

five-story building on the north side of the square that extended along Sixth Street between Vine and Walnut Streets and housed parking and executives. The office tower became known as DuBois Tower, and DuBois Chemical Company put its headquarters in the building. Fifth Third Bank moved from its headquarters at the northwest corner of Fourth and Walnut Streets to occupy the five-story executive office building and also four floors in the larger tower.

The 1969 redesign was deemed a great success upon its completion. Edmund Bacon, the eminent Philadelphia urban planner, called it "the most successful public Square in America." In 1974, the American Institute of Architects bestowed its Honor Award, its highest award for achievement in architectural design, upon the project. The AIA commented that the new square was "another successful example in a growing number of public

Fountain Square was rededicated on October 18, 1969; this photograph was taken shortly after the reopening. The DuBois Tower (now the Fifth Third Tower) to the left and the Tri-State Building to the back right are still present in 2013. The Sheraton Gibson Hotel on the right ceased operation in 1974 and was demolished in 1977. *Courtesy of Cincinnati Museum Center–Cincinnati Historical Society Library.*

Cincinnati was home to many breweries both before and after Prohibition. This parade entrant was sponsored by Burger Beer, which operated from 1934 until 1973, when it closed and sold its recipes and trademarks to the Hudepohl Brewing Company. The sign on the cart pays homage to Cincinnati's German heritage when it asks, "Vas You Efer in Zinzinnati?" *Courtesy of Cincinnati Museum Center–Cincinnati Historical Society Library.*

Squares causing our cities to be more enjoyable places" and a "sign of the will of the city to save itself." Of the redesigned square, one writer observed in 1985 that

> *in the mid-1960s, when the new Fountain Square was conceived, the idea was to create an informal outdoor gathering space which could serve as the symbolic center of the city.*
>
> *Fountain Square became the embodiment of that ideal...The goal was also realized here because Fountain Square was in the traditional center of the city, across from the Carew Tower arcade at Fifth and Vine Sts., and because the historic Tyler Davidson Fountain was retained as its centerpiece.*
>
> *The fountain is the closest thing to a city symbol we have. And because it has been around for a while—more than 100 years—it has worked its way*

> *into the hearts and mind of the citizens. Like other 19th-century sculptures, it conforms to what people's expectations of what a public monument ought to be.*
>
> *Everybody loves Fountain Square, and in good weather, especially at lunch time, it is filled to overflowing. It has served as a catalyst for redevelopment downtown.*

The 1969 redesign focused on the new Fountain Square Plaza and the buildings surrounding the plaza, but it did not focus on upkeep, cleaning and rehabilitation of the nearly century-old fountain itself. Instead the planners determined to clean and maintain the fountain to have the Genius of Water ready for its centennial in 1971. Frederick Hauck agreed to pay for the work, and Eleftheiros Karkadoulias, a Greek immigrant, was hired to clean one hundred years of dirt off the fountain, to fix more than one hundred cracks and to restore the patina. On October 6, 1971, one hundred years to the day since the fountain was first dedicated by the fountain's donor, Henry Probasco, his eighty-three-year-old daughter, Grace Probasco Rowe, cut the white ribbon to unveil the restored fountain. Attending the ceremony were Richard Haupt, director of the Cincinnati Historical Society; William S. Rowe, grandson of Henry Probasco and chairman of the centennial committee; and John Gilligan, Ohio governor.

A short-lived visitor to the new Fountain Square was the sculpture *Law and Society*, which was placed at the corner of Fifth and Walnut Streets during parts of 1972 and 1973. Charles Sawyer, a partner at Taft Stettinius & Hollister and formerly secretary of commerce in the administration of President Harry S. Truman, was prevailed upon to donate $25,000 to commission the sculpture in honor of the 100th anniversary of the Cincinnati Bar Association. A five-member committee—which did not include Sawyer but did include the curator of the Cincinnati Art Museum and other art patrons and enthusiasts—selected the design of sculptor Barna Von Sartory, of Berlin, over thirty other applicants. The sculpture consists of a thirty-four-ton chunk of Indiana limestone atop a square-shouldered, stainless steel arch. The statue was instantly mocked and derided. After less than one year on Fountain Square, the sculpture was moved to the new 14½-acre Sawyer Point Park on the Ohio River. This park was made possible by Sawyer's $1 million gift to the city to buy the land.

The new Fountain Square's original design had a portable stage in its northeast corner that was used for speeches and concerts, but it was deemed inadequate for its intended use, so a large, forty-nine-foot-tall, forty-five-foot-wide Fountain Square Pavilion clad in rose granite was inaugurated in that northeast corner space on August 8, 1985, with a performance by Donny and Marie Osmond. Frederick Hauck gave a significant amount for the stage's construction, and the funds to build it were privately raised. Later, however, many thought that the stage was too large and detracted from the centerpiece of the square—the fountain. The stage was cited by many as one of the reasons why the square should be redone in 2005.

Twenty-nine years after the fountain had been rehabilitated, by 2000 it again was in need of restoration. Private funds were raised to make the necessary improvements, and yet another dedication of the fountain was held that year to commemorate its restoration to service.

Chapter 8

Fountain Square, Version 3

The Fountain Faces South, 2006–Present

By 2003, the 1969 Fountain Square Plaza redesign, which had earned so much favorable comment when it opened, was criticized as "cold and brutal." The plaza was deemed outdated, and the layout and design, originally viewed as a passive, urban oasis, was seen thirty-four years later as unwelcoming and harsh. The granite seat benches around most of the square's perimeter were viewed as a type of fence, keeping people from entering the square. The 1985 performance stage was called "hulking" and obstructed the center of the square. The roof of the parking garage built in 1966 leaked, and its structural integrity was in jeopardy. Critics of the square's design believed that "the Fountain had turned into a drive-by attraction instead of a destination where visitors could gather, linger and enjoy the city."

The Fountain Square Working Group, led by Federated Department Stores CEO Jim Zimmerman, managed the renovation for 3CDC, the Cincinnati Center City Development Corporation. The task force hired John Alschuler, a New York consultant, to try to draft a plan that would create a "destination" feeling for the square with more shopping and dining. At the time the plan was drafted, there was but a single restaurant on the square. The plan called for the elimination of the skywalk from the square across Vine Street, removal of the stage and elimination of the wall of granite seating to make it easier for pedestrians to access the square. The plan also called for the fountain to move, again, this time closer to the middle of the plaza, and to have the Genius of Water face south. The plan also called for the building of a restaurant on the square above the Vine Street parking ramp, as well as the necessary renovations to the garage itself.

The *Enquirer* noted that "there is bound to be resistance to altering the Square's basic appearance. The Fountain itself is one of the dominant features of the downtown streetscape, and its stage has hosted events ranging from U.S. presidential campaign stops to World Series victory rallies." It then quoted Mayor Charlie Luken, who stated: "Fountain Square is sacred to most Cincinnatians. I know people have historic attachments to the Square, but I think it needs to happen. I think the time is right."

The cost to rehabilitate the garage and redo the Fountain Square Plaza was $48.9 million—the city put in $4 million and the balance was funded privately through various sources. The project started in October 2005, and the square was closed for the better part of a year. The Genius of Water was moved about one hundred feet north and closer to the center of the

The fountain was moved again, courtesy of the 2006 renovations, to almost the center of the plaza that originally was created as a part of the 1969 rework of Fountain Square. With this move, the Genius of Water faces south directly onto Fifth Street. The Fifth Third Bank offices are shown in this photo behind the fountain. The "wall of glass" in front of those offices was also added as part of the 2006 renovation. *Courtesy of J. Miles Wolf.*

The Via Vite restaurant was built and opened as part of the 2006 Fountain Square revitalization project. *Courtesy of the author.*

square. She now faces south, looking over the square and directly onto Fifth Street. The garage was redone. The Fifth Third executive office building added sheets of glass covering the exterior for a new modern look. Lights that change color were installed behind the glass sheets. The restaurant built on the square's northwest corner was leased by Via Vite, operated by Nicola and Christian Pietoso. New bars and restaurants opened on the first floor of the thirty-two-story Fifth Third tower and on the first floor of the Fifth Third executive office building.

The *Cincinnati Enquirer* reported on the occasion of the 2006 rededication that

> *the city...and other key players downtown say the revamped square will usher in a new era of vitality and growth in a core area that's faced challenges as businesses and people fled to the suburbs. "I don't think you can overestimate the psychic importance of Fountain Square as the heart of the city and the entire region," said David Ginsburg, president and CEO of Downtown Cincinnati Inc., the organization that promotes downtown as a good place to live, work and shop.*

The Fountain Square renovation did, in fact, open the era in which a substantial part of downtown—the banks along the Ohio River and Over-the-

Cincinnati has been known as the Queen City since 1819. Henry Wadsworth Longfellow memorialized the Queen City expression in the final stanza of his poem "Catawba Wine," which was etched into marble and placed in the square when it was refinished in 2006. *Courtesy of the author.*

Rhine—were also revitalized with new condominiums, apartments, restaurants and bars throughout. Demand for apartment space in both areas is particularly high among both recent college graduates and new empty nesters.

Boosters of the city of Cincinnati have been calling it the "Queen City" since 1819, when B. Cooke stated in the *Cincinnati Advertiser* that "the city is, indeed, justly styled the fair Queen of the West: distinguished for order, enterprise, public spirit and liberality, she stands the wonder of an admiring world." Henry Wadsworth Longfellow memorialized the Queen City expression in his poem "Catawba Wine," which memorializes the city's vineyards, including especially those of Cincinnati's first prominent citizen, Nicholas Longworth. The final stanza of the poem is:

> *And this Song of the Vine,*
> *This greeting of mine,*
> *The winds and the birds shall deliver,*
> *To the Queen of the West,*
> *In her garlands dressed,*
> *On the banks of the Beautiful River.*

Broomball is played weeknights during January and February on the square's outdoor ice skating rink, which is the largest in the United States after the one in Rockefeller Center. The game is played like hockey, with running shoes and a ball instead of skates and a puck. *Courtesy of the author.*

The 2006 renovation of the square also found a way to imprint this as this stanza is inscribed on a water wall on the square, just to the east of the Genius of Water.

The rededication ceremony for the new Fountain Square was held on October 14, 2006. After seven years, the renovation of the plaza has been a stunning success. Tens of thousands of people turn out to watch the summer music series, and tens of thousands more people take advantage of the largest urban skating rink outside of New York City for figure skating and broomball from December through February.

Chapter 9

The Carew Building, the Carew Tower and the Emery Family

Introduction

The Carew Tower complex, at the southwest corner of Fifth and Vine Streets, has been Cincinnati's most recognizable set of buildings since its completion in 1931. It was one of the nation's first "city within a city" complexes that combined an office tower with retail space, a hotel and a parking garage. Notably, the entire complex was completed in less than fourteen months from the time of its groundbreaking. The public spaces in the office tower and hotel are Art Deco masterpieces that still resonate today.

Original Buildings and Gradual Gentrification

The Carew Tower was not built until almost sixty years after the city and Henry Probasco made the original Fountain Square. When the fountain was dedicated in 1871, the buildings surrounding Fountain Square reflected the sort of neighborhood where the noxious Fifth Street Market had stood for many years until 1870. At the corner where the Carew Tower stands today, a series of small buildings, home to several small stores, was present. The fountain and Fountain Square proved to have a gentrifying effect on the area.

Thomas Emery's Sons

The sons of Thomas W. Emery began the gentrification process on this street corner. Thomas W. Emery, an immigrant from England, arrived in Cincinnati in 1830 near the beginning of Cincinnati's rapid population growth. He opened a loan office and also a real estate office, which bought more land than it sold. Emery then branched out in 1840 into lard oil, starting the Emery Candle Company that made dripless candles for sale. Emery passed away in 1857, leaving substantial debts. Two of his sons, Thomas J. Emery (1828–1906) and John J. Emery (1827–1908), used the unsold land left by their father and also the money generated from the Emery Candle Company to build the beginning of an empire. They paid their father's debts, and through their Thomas Emery's Sons Company, they became the biggest landowners in Ohio. John and Thomas Emery also owned and developed property throughout the country.

In 1875—four years after the Fountain Square dedication—Thomas Emery's Sons began acquiring land on Fifth Street between Vine and Race Streets, and in 1877, they built the Emery Hotel, with 176 rooms, on the corner of Fifth and Race Streets where the hotel part of the Carew Tower complex is now. In 1889, Joseph T. Carew (1848–1914) continued the gentrification process when he built the Carew Building directly on the corner Fifth and Vine, an eleven-story tower that he connected to the Emery Hotel. The Carew Building had a two-story, glass-enclosed retail atrium that linked Race Street with Vine Street. The arcade was home to seventy shops and stores. Also on this block were the Andrews Building, the Emery Hotel and a number of smaller buildings.

The Emery Hotel, with 176 rooms, was built at the corner of Fifth and Race Streets by Thomas Emery's Sons Co. in 1877. The fountain and Fountain Square proved to have a gentrifying effect on the immediate neighborhood. *Courtesy of the Public Library of Cincinnati and Hamilton County.*

Thomas Emery established the Cincinnati Orphan Asylum, and he was a large contributor to the Colored

The lobby of the Emery Hotel, where the gentlemen wore suits, ties and hats. *Courtesy of the Public Library of Cincinnati and Hamilton County.*

This photograph from the early 1900s shows the Mabley & Carew building (near right), the Carew Building (with the clock face) and the Rollman Department Store Building (the light-colored building to the left hand of the Genius of Water). *Courtesy of Cincinnati Museum Center–Cincinnati Historical Society Library.*

This two-story arcade, clad in glass and iron, connected the Carew Building on Vine Street with the Emery Hotel from 1889 until 1929. The arcade was home to more than seventy merchants. *Courtesy of Cincinnati Museum Center–Cincinnati Historical Society Library.*

Orphans Asylum. He also worked with Booker T. Washington (1856–1915) in Washington's educational work. Among many notable pursuits, Washington was the first leader of the Tuskegee Institute in Alabama, whose mission was to educate African Americans.

Thomas Emery died while visiting Cairo, Egypt, leaving approximately $20 million to his wife, Mary. Mary Muhlenberg Hopkins (1844–1927) had two sons, Sheldon (1867–1890) and Albert (1868–1884), with Emery, but they had died young. When Thomas died in 1906, leaving Mary a widow and alone, she remained active in the community. She supported the Cincinnati Zoo, donated an entire wing to the Cincinnati Art Museum and was one of the founders of Cincinnati Children's Hospital Medical Center.

She was appalled by the unsanitary housing conditions of those living downtown, and so she founded the planned community Mariemont in suburban Cincinnati. Her son Sheldon's friend Charles Livingood hired John Nolen to plan Mariemont, and Nolen's blueprint was developed from 1920 to 1925. Mary Emery's death in 1927 and the Great Depression, which began in 1929, slowed the building of the village, but eventually the community was fully built. Today, it is one of the city's model communities. Ironically, the village, planned in large part for working-class people, did not reach this aim but instead today is home to lawyers, doctors and business executives.

Jack Emery

John "Jack" Josiah Emery (1878–1976), the son of John J. and Lela Emery, then entered the story. Emery was born in New York City and was educated at Groton, Harvard and Trinity College at Oxford University. Emery stated that "I was just going to go into the publishing business…in 1924, but I came out [to Cincinnati] to look around. I found that the Emery Candle Company was just a grease factory with obsolete equipment and a sort of Dickensian office. I decided the family was going to go bust if someone didn't hang around and fix things up."

Fix things up he did. Jack Emery turned the Emery Candle Company into the Emery Chemical Company, later the Emery Oleochemical Group, a specialty chemical manufacturer that today has thirteen worldwide plants. He became president of the real estate development company Thomas Emery's Sons, Inc. in 1925. He also became one of Cincinnati's most important civic boosters. He served for fifty years as a trustee of the Cincinnati Art Museum, sparked the creation of the Fine Arts Fund (now known as ArtsWave), was a founder of the Cincinnati Country Day School, served as trustee of the Cincinnati Children's Home and was quite active in the local Boy Scouts. Thomas Emery's Sons built the Cincinnatian Hotel and the Terrace Plaza Hotel.

Jack Emery also built Peterloon, a twelve-hundred-acre estate, in Indian Hill. Emery and his wife, Irene, the daughter of artist Charles Dana Gibson, built the English-style country home. The house is four stories, built in the Georgian–Queen Anne style. It has thirty-six rooms, twenty-one bathrooms and nineteen fireplaces. It took two years to build and was finished by 1930. William Delàno, a cousin of then–New York governor Franklin Delano Roosevelt, was the architect. The *Cincinnati Enquirer* reports that "Peterloon's massive living room, dining room and library have paneling and flooring from 17th and 18th century British and French houses. A carved 16th-century stone fireplace in the entrance foyer is the oldest piece built into the structure." Today, the Emery Foundation owns the house and grounds and maintains it "for the benefit, avocation and enjoyment of the Greater Cincinnati community." To this end, it hosts forty-five to fifty events per year, including numerous weddings.

Carew Tower Development with Walter Starrett

In the late 1920s, the Thomas Emery Corporation, successor to Thomas Emery's Sons, Inc., bought the Carew Building and the other buildings on the block where the Carew Tower is today. Once Jack Emery was finished buying up this land across from Fountain Square, he announced the development of the Carew Tower on August 24, 1929, in a deal between the Thomas Emery Corporation and the Starrett Investment Corporation, which was operated by Walter Starrett.

In the 1920s, Starrett demolished the original Waldorf-Astoria Hotel and erected the Empire State Building in its place, putting it up at the rate of one story per day and completing the job in 1931 at $2 million, less than the original estimate. Starrett also built the Lincoln Memorial and Union Station in Washington, D.C., and Penn Station in New York. Starrett, originally from Kansas City, trained at Burnham and Root in Chicago. In 1928, he wrote the seminal treatise *Skyscrapers and the Men Who Build Them.* He was one of these men. In his book, he describes the transformative effect that skyscrapers could have on a city. He states:

> *One singular and significant fact of skyscraper construction here stands out, and that is its power fairly to move centres of cities. Under the old order, the crossroads, vast traffic streams and dense population knew no law but itself...but now it is different. Great structures can actually beckon the trends of population and traffic, and in a measure can compel the shifting of economic centres of gravity.*

The deal that was eventually reached between Emery and Starrett called for a $15 million project made up of a forty-eight-story office tower, five levels of retail space within the tower, a twenty-nine-story hotel and a twenty-eight-story parking garage. Walter Ahlschlager, a noted Chicago architect who designed the Peabody Hotel in Memphis and the Roxy Theatre in New York City, was hired to design the complex. Edgar Brandt, a Frenchman, was hired to do the interior design. His work featured "frozen" fountains, rams' horns and other Art Deco devices that could be easily produced. This was of keen interest to Starrett, who wished to see the complex constructed quickly. George Unger also is credited with much of the interior design work.

This drawing depicts the Carew Tower on the left and the Netherland Plaza hotel on the right, with space for retail at the base of the complex. The set of buildings, finished in 1931, was one of the first "city within a city" complexes in the United States, which combined space for office, hotel, retail and parking. The sign for the Netherland Plaza is grossly out of scale. *Courtesy of the Public Library of Cincinnati and Hamilton County.*

The timing of the August 24, 1929 announcement of the Carew Tower project proved fortunate for Jack Emery. In order to generate the cash to pay for his share of the project, he liquidated much of the family's stocks and securities in the summer of 1929 against the advice of his financial advisors. Had he waited until the Great Depression began on Black Friday—October 29, 1929—much of the family fortune likely would have been lost in the stock market and the Carew Tower may never have been built. Starrett met the opposite fate as Emery, for he was heavily invested in the market and in properties that could not be leased. He ended up selling his interest in the complex back to the Emerys in November 1932.

Starrett's "fast track" construction technique worked marvelously on the complex. The project was announced in August 1929, and ground was broken in January 1930. The Mabley & Carew Department Store, which leased five stories in the office tower for its retail space, was open for business in October 1930. The Netherland Plaza hotel opened in January 1931, and the parking garage opened on February 10, 1931. The 574-foot-tall retail/ office tower was Cincinnati's tallest building from the time of its completion until 2010, when the Great American Tower at Queen City Square was built at Third and Sycamore Streets.

By 1928, downtown Cincinnati was rated the third-most congested city in the nation. Starrett's plan for the Carew Tower complex sought to minimize traffic congestion on the streets by offering as many services as possible within the three buildings, thus reducing the need for patrons to travel from building to building by car. This plan included room for a department store, an arcade for smaller shops, a cafeteria, a post office, a coffee shop, hair salons and office space. The complex was the first to have underground freight loading and unloading space so that trucks would not need to park on the street and create traffic congestion. The hotel had eight hundred guest rooms, a wedding chapel, large ballrooms—including the fabulous Hall of Mirrors—and a power plant. The twenty-eight-story, 750-car parking garage, though, was one of a kind: it was fully automated. Drivers pulled into the garage and left the car on an automated platform that would then move the car into an open space in the garage. The car would be returned to the driver in the same fashion. The automated system did not last long. It was designed for overnight hotel guests, not for those who would come in and out simply to go shopping, and so congestion ensued. Mechanical breakdowns of the equipment also caused problems. Eventually, people were hired to take the cars up and down on the lifts. Over time, road salt eroded the structural steel supports, and the garage later was demolished in the mid-1980s. Today, the Tower Place shopping complex sits where the parking garage once stood.

As construction was drawing to a close, Emery chose the name St. Nicholas Plaza for the project; however, the Cincinnati Realty Company claimed to own this name as it had bought the rights to it from the then closed St. Nicholas Hotel at Fourth and Race Streets. An injunction was issued against Emery from using the name, but it came after all linens, china, silverware and stationery with the "St. NP" monograms had been purchased. Another name with these initials was needed, and so the St. Netherland Plaza name was adopted, with the "St." eventually dropped.

The hotel and tower are decorated in the Art Deco style, and this theme is especially apparent in the Netherland Plaza. There, decorations of antelope, giant sea horses, lotus flowers and Egyptian themes are present. The Palm Court restaurant and bar (space that originally was the main lobby) constitute what is arguably the most elegant and interesting public space in the city.

This space was the original lobby for the Netherland Plaza hotel. Today, the Palm Court bar and restaurant and the Orchids restaurant (in the foreground) occupy what is arguably the most elegant room in Cincinnati. *Courtesy of J. Miles Wolf.*

There are ten murals in the Palm Court by Louis Grell done in Louis XV fashion. Each depicts actors in leisure or recreation, and each also depicts the Carew Tower mixed somewhere in the background. The fountain and sea horses were made at Rookwood Pottery. The center arcade of the office tower is notably decorated in many respects with a variety of Art Deco touches. Found there are two enormous archways decorated by Rookwood Tile in a design by William Hentschel (1892–1962). Hentschel was a well-known ceramic designer and artist for over forty years at Rookwood Pottery and the Art Academy of Cincinnati. His Rookwood tile work can also be seen at the entrance to Dixie Terminal and the Rookwood Tea Room at Union Terminal. His Rookwood arches in the Carew Tower, based on a repeating design by Parisian metalsmith Edgar Brandt, are some of the largest Rookwood tile installations in the world.

Mabley & Carew was the department store tenant in the Carew Tower until 1962, when it moved to the northwest corner of Fifth and Vine to a building it owned. H.S. Pogue's Stores, which had its main store at Fourth and Race, then took over the retail department store space in the Carew

The Carew Tower arcade mimics the arcade that connected the Carew Building and Hotel Emery and that was in the same place as this arcade. Mabley & Carew, and later Pogue's, leased the retail shopping space from 1931 until 1988. The two-story Rookwood tile arch depicted at the end of the arcade is one of the largest Rookwood installations in the world. *Courtesy of Cincinnati Museum Center–Cincinnati Historical Society Library.*

Tower for twenty-two years until Pogue's was merged into L.S. Ayres in 1984. L.S. Ayres eventually went defunct in 1988. Other longtime tenants of Carew Tower have included the venerable Hathaway's Coffee Shop, Thoma Opticians, Appointments and Hunt Club Clothiers. Generations of downtown office workers have eaten their lunch at Mabley & Carew, Hathaway's and the Netherland Plaza restaurants.

After fifty years, the tower complex had become dated. In 1981, the Emerys decided to spend $28 million to renovate and restore the complex, and the number of hotel rooms was reduced to 624 in order to make many rooms larger. Before the renovation was complete in 1990, the Emerys sold the complex to the Belvedere Corporation on the condition that Belvedere finish the restoration work. Belvedere finished that work in 1992, and it also built the three-story Tower Place Mall on the sites of the former parking garage and the former Pogue's building at Fourth

The Carew Tower (foreground) and Netherland Plaza (back right) as they appear in 2013. The Fountain Square skating rink is in the foreground. The stage is behind the ice rink, and it is used by musical acts in warmer weather. *Courtesy of the author.*

and Race Streets. Belvedere did another major renovation to the hotel in 2004, and the number of guest rooms in the hotel was reduced again, this time to 561.

The United States Department of the Interior's National Register of Historic Places recognized the tower for its historical value in 1983. The complex was designated a National Historic Landmark in 1994. Among the many famous visitors to the hotel have been Winston Churchill, Elvis Presley, Eleanor Roosevelt, Bing Crosby and President George H.W. Bush.

Chapter 10

Fountain Square North

Block A

Fountain Square was dedicated in October 1871, and it lay in the middle of a divided Fifth Street that was open to traffic going both east and west. This chapter discusses the stores and buildings on the north part of Fifth Street between Vine and Walnut Streets. This block would later become labeled by the city as the "A" block in its 1960s revitalization plans.

The department store that would become known as Mabley & Carew was started by Detroit merchants C.R. Mabley and Joseph T. Carew in 1877, six years after the fountain dedication. They built their six-floor store on the northeast corner of Fifth and Vine Streets in 1881, immediately north of Fountain Square.

Carew, a Canadian, had moved to Detroit as a young man and found a place there with C.R. Mabley in the Star Clothing House. Mabley recognized Carew as an up-and-comer and moved him to Cincinnati in 1877 to manage another of Mabley's department stores. Mabley made Carew a partner in 1881, and Carew started the Mabley & Carew department store at the northeast corner of Fifth and Vine Streets that year. Carew was noted to be "among the first to recognize the value of extensive advertising and judicious catering to the demands of the public." The *Cincinnati Enquirer* obituary for him, published December 12, 1914, describes a remarkable man:

> *One of Cincinnati's most distinguished citizens answered the long roll call yesterday. For more than a third of a century, Joseph Thomas Carew has been identified with all that was best and most progressive in the*

development and growth of the city of his adoptions. Self-made in the best sense of the oft-abused term, he succeeded without tyranny and achieved without arrogance.

With fine generosity, and withal with splendid business foresight, he guided his employees along the tortuous pathway he himself had blazed, binding them to himself and to the great business he had developed with bonds of steel by giving them such interest in the business as their capacity and endeavor justified. He pioneered in modern advertising methods, which splendidly rewarded and vindicated his business judgment.

Deeply sensible of civic duty and responsibility, he steadfastly declined public office, although repeated effort was made to thrust such honor upon him. It is no secret that he might have been the Republican nominee for governor of Ohio had he given his consent, nor that his party had repeatedly importuned him to accept the mayoralty nomination. In either or any official capacity, his genius for business and organization would have won him high acclaim, but he preferred to work out his public debt through personal channels of his own choosing.

The impress of his kindly, genial demeanor, his energy and business methods, will be lasting, and imperishable monument to his memory in the hearts of those who knew him. Cincinnati can ill afford to lose men of the type of Joseph T. Carew.

Mabley & Carew stayed on this corner for forty-nine years, until 1930, when it moved into the retail space available in the new Carew Tower. In 1957, the owners of the original Mabley & Carew Building lopped off its top three floors, which had been vacant for years. The Spritz Department Store moved into the "new" three-story building in late summer 1957. Spritz was founded as a clothing establishment in 1931 and twenty-five years later had branched out to become a full-service department store. There were eight other storefronts, as well as a theater, on the northside Fifth Street block between Vine and Walnut Streets ranging from two to six stories.

The 1881 Mabley & Carew Building was bought by the city in 1965 so that it could be demolished as part of the Fountain Square revitalization project. A jury set the price at $476,200. The underground parking garage under Fountain Square was built under the site of the former department store.

The Fountain Square building, a sixteen-story office building with retail space, was located on the northwest corner of Fifth and Walnut. It was built in 1928 and demolished in 1966 as part of the revitalization project. The

Daily Commercial called this building "one of the outstanding show places of the city." The Fountain Square building was half the size it was originally planned to be, however; the builders could not get all the land they wanted, so the lot on which they built the sixteen-story building was only 33 feet deep behind a 100-foot frontage on Walnut Street. Builders touted the building, at 203 feet, as "easily the tallest structure in the vicinity" with "light and air on four sides" and as a unique one-floor/one-tenant plan for occupancy.

In 1950, the Fraternal Order of Eagles acquired the land and the building on which the Fountain Square building was situated for $1.5 million. The Eagles bought the building as an investment and made no changes whatsoever for the building's management. Fifteen years later, the city spent $1 million for this final piece of the Fountain Square puzzle to make room for the DuBois Tower and the Fifth Third executive office building.

The tenants in the building, which included the Maisonette, LaNormandie, Queen City Flowers, Discount Records and Jacob Jewelers, were all displaced by the city's 1965 purchase.

Chapter II

Fountain Square South

Block B

Fountain Square South, the block immediately south of the square on Fifth Street, has seen two different scenes over the past 142 years. The first scene saw the Gibson Hotel, the Albee Theatre, several small office and retail buildings, the building housing the Wiggins Restaurant on Fifth Street and the Fountain Square Hotel on Vine Street. These structures were demolished in 1977 to make room for the second scene that housed the twenty-six-story First National Bank Center (now the U.S. Bank Tower) and the seventeen-story Westin Hotel, which opened in 1981.

The Gibson Hotel first occupied the southwest corner of Fifth and Walnut Streets beginning in 1849, twenty-two years before the first Fountain Square was dedicated. The first hotel closed after one year because it was too far out in the country. It reopened shortly thereafter and remained open until 1873, when it was razed to be replaced by a larger hotel. The second Gibson Hotel operated until 1912, when it was destroyed by fire. The third Gibson Hotel, a twelve-story building, lasted until 1922. At that point, it was substantially enlarged to become "the largest hostelry in the Midwest" with one thousand rooms. When it first opened, the Fountain Square Gibson had ten floors with one hundred rooms each. When the Netherland Plaza opened in 1931, this provided eighteen hundred rooms between the two hotels that were just one block apart. Sheraton Corporation bought the Gibson Hotel in 1950 and renamed it the Sheraton Gibson.

There were four entrances to the main lobby of the 1923 Gibson. The main entrance was on Walnut Street, and a second entry, the ladies' entrance, was

Right: This twelve-story version of the Gibson Hotel, seen from Fifth Street, as it appeared from 1912 to 1922. *Courtesy of the Public Library of Cincinnati and Hamilton County.*

Below: The Gibson Hotel, built in 1923 and depicted between 1927, when the Albee Theater opened, and 1929. The Carew Building, which was demolished at the end of that year, is evident at the far right. Fountain Square is in the foreground. When the Gibson opened it was the "largest hostelry in the Midwest," with one thousand rooms. The hotel closed in 1974 and was demolished in 1977 to make room for the First National Bank Center, which is today U.S. Bank Tower. *Courtesy of the Public Library of Cincinnati and Hamilton County.*

just north of the main entrance. The third entrance was on Fourth Street, down a long white marble corridor to the hotel. The fourth entrance was at the rear of the Union Trust building (today's Bartlett Building) on Fourth and Walnut Streets.

The Gibson had a luxurious lounge just west of the lobby. The main dining room, the Florentine Dining Room, was two stories. The mezzanine of the restaurant, which overlooked Fountain Square, was reached from the dining room's Grand Staircase. At the Gibson's eventual closing, one writer for the *Cincinnati Post* recalled that "the Florentine Room, the main dining room, was of such elegance that it gave the feeling of a palace in which Mona Lisa was in residence. Soft lights, marble columns, gleaming silver, pristine crystal, snowy napkins—and the food was famous." The ballroom and banquet space on the floor above the mezzanine covered 3,700 square feet, and it had banquet space for 1,200 people. The Gibson had a rooftop garden enclosed entirely in glass that extended the entire Fifth Street length of the hotel. This room, called the Gibson Room, could seat 1,500 guests. A *Cincinnati Post* reporter recalled that "before World War II, Halloween and New Year's Eve were supposed to be spent on Fountain Square, which meant the Gibson was involved. Normally drunk people waved floor lamps out of upper stories. It was fun."

Later, the Gibson saw the Lobby Lounge re-created as the Yeatman's Cove bar. In 1965, the Florentine Room was restyled as the Kon Tiki, a restaurant featuring "oriental cooking with a Polynesian flair, the likes of which Cincinnati has never seen," according to promotional materials. The hotel hosted fifty-four governors from the United States and its territories in 1968 for the National Governors Conference. Ronald Reagan of California, Spiro Agnew of Maryland, Nelson Rockefeller of New York and George Romney of Michigan were among those attending. In July 1970, the brand-new Riverfront Stadium hosted Major League Baseball's All-Star game, and the Gibson ballroom was home to dinner for the officials of the National and American Leagues.

The Gibson remained open until July 15, 1974. The writing on the wall came with the information that the block was going to be redeveloped with an office tower and a new hotel.

The Wiggins Restaurant occupied the southeast corner of Fifth and Vine Streets, on the first floor of a six-story building. One regular reported that Wiggins "was the sort of downtown establishment where the regulars had their own booths and the waitresses knew everybody's business. A lot of people used Wiggins as a surrogate family. It was a meal with friends, served by people you knew." The offices above the restaurant housed any number of tenants. These included the law firm of Worthington & Strong, a predecessor to Taft Stettinius & Hollister, whose offices were in Rooms 25–27 in the Wiggins building. Wiggins served its last meal on December

The exterior of the Albee Theater on the south side of Fifth Street facing Fountain Square as it appeared from December 24, 1927, until 1977. The arch was moved before demolition to the Cincinnati Convention Center. *Courtesy of Cincinnati Museum Center–Cincinnati Historical Society Library.*

31, 1974, and moved to Wiggins Other Place at 34 East Fourth Street. The office building that housed Wiggins was demolished in the summer of 1977 to make room for the new Fountain Square South.

There were several minor buildings in the middle of the southside Fifth Street block as well, which housed a number of small businesses.

The RKO Albee Theater sat between the Wiggins Restaurant and the Gibson Hotel. The $4 million palatial theater opened on Christmas Eve 1927. It was named for its builder, E.F. Albee, a vaudeville theater owner. The Palace, the Grand and the Lyric were other notable downtown theaters, but the Albee was the gem of these. The Albee's exterior featured a gorgeous marble façade. It was lushly appointed with twin marble staircases, a forty- by seventy-foot carpeted foyer, crystal chandeliers and oil paintings. It had the Mighty Wurlitzer organ, and the theater itself was huge, seating 3,500 people, just slightly fewer than the Music Hall.

The Albee was built both for movies and for live vaudeville shows and musical acts. Throughout the 1940s, weekend crowds were standing room only

The main stage of the Albee, complete with an orchestra pit for musicians. The stage curtain is the height of three stories. *Courtesy of Cincinnati Museum Center–Cincinnati Historical Society Library.*

This photograph shows the interior seating of the Albee. The theater seated 3,500 people, only slightly fewer than Cincinnati Music Hall in Over-the-Rhine. It was built to host live shows and movies. *Courtesy of Cincinnati Museum Center–Cincinnati Historical Society Library.*

on Saturdays and Sundays, but by the end of the 1950s, the live shows came to an end. The last movie was shown in 1974 when the theater closed. Public objection to its razing kept the Albee around until 1977 as attempts to sell it for demolishment and reconstruction were fought by many, but these objections came to naught when no practical use for its revival was found. The Albee was demolished in 1977 as part of the Fountain Square South project. The Mighty Wurlitzer organ eventually made its way to the Music Hall ballroom, along with many pieces of the theater's architectural fixtures and artifacts. The magnificent, exterior marble façade was kept intact and was placed on the Fifth Street side of the Cincinnati Convention Center, where it remains today.

The twelve-story Fountain Square Hotel was situated on Vine Street immediately south of the Wiggins Building, its southern wall ending at an alley

A stairway leading to the balcony and mezzanine of the Albee. *Courtesy of Cincinnati Museum Center–Cincinnati Historical Society Library.*

that separated the hotel from the Ingalls Building on Fourth Street. The Ingalls Building was the United States' first steel-reinforced concrete skyscraper, constructed in 1903, and the fifteen-story building still stands today. The Fountain Square Hotel had 250 rooms with a "bath and radio in every room."

It featured the Purple Cow Sandwich Shop and the Beautiful Music Box Café. It remained until 1977.

A depiction of the Fountain Square Hotel facing Vine Street, with Fifth Street shown to the top of the image. The hotel had 250 rooms and promised a "bath and radio in very room." The office, retail and restaurant building housing the Wiggins restaurant is shown attached to the hotel and in front of Fifth and Vine Streets. Both buildings were demolished in 1977 to make room for the U.S. Bank Tower and Westin Hotel complex that opened in 1981. *Courtesy of Don Prout.*

Once the city had finished with the 1969 version of the new Fountain Square, DuBois Tower and the Fifth Third office building, it next set its eyes on the redevelopment of Fountain Square South, or what the city revitalization plans called "Block B." Once the Sheraton Gibson closed on July 15, 1974, the writing was on the wall for the entire block. The Albee closed later that year, and the Wiggins Restaurant served its last meal on December 31, 1974. The city gave some of the smaller tenants—Central Progressive Savings Association, the European Health Spa, Gibson Paper Place, John's Tie Shop, Saxony Imports, Lomark Discount Drugs, Fannie Farmer Candies and B-G Meal-A-Minute Diner—until March 31, 1975, to vacate.

The city plan in 1976 was to build a fifteen- to eighteen-story luxury hotel that would be operated by Western International Hotels and a twenty-nine-story office tower where the First National Bank of Cincinnati would be the lead tenant. The John W. Galbreath Company was hired to develop the property. Land acquisition costs of $7 million were estimated, including $1.1 million for the Wiggins building, $2 million for the Albee and the Fountain

The U.S. Bank Tower and Westin Hotel complex as it appears on the south side of Fifth Street in 2013. *Courtesy of the author.*

Square Hotel, $3.3 million for the Sheraton Gibson and $455,000 for two small parcels. Demolition began in 1977, but a 111-day strike by Laborers Local 265 put the project behind schedule from the very beginning.

The First National Bank of Cincinnati agreed on February 28, 1978, to become the prime tenant and one of the investors in the twenty-six-story office tower, along with Galbreath and an insurance company mortgage holder. The size of the office tower was scaled back from the original plan for a twenty-nine-story tower for fear the supply of the extra three floors would outstrip demand. But demand for the 560,000 square feet in the tower found it almost fully leased for its January 1981 opening. Tenants included Taft Stettinius & Hollister, Coldwell Banker, Johnson & Higgins, Peck Shaffer & Williams, Rolf & Rolf, Paine Webber Jackson & Curtis, Merrill Lynch Pierce Fenner & Smith, Hartford Insurance, Deloitte Haskins & Sells, Hurdman & Cransoun, Chubb & Sons and Meidinger & Associates. Gidding Jenny's Men's Store occupied the two retail floors in the office tower, and First National Bank's main branch was located on the first floor, as well. The office tower has seen a number of name changes as the First National Bank of Cincinnati changed its name to Star Bank in 1988, then to Firstar Bank in 1998 and then to U.S. Bank in 2001. The name of the office tower changed on each occasion.

The seventeen-story luxury hotel opened in March 1981. Western International changed its name to Westin Hotels in early 1981, and this hotel was the first to carry the new name. Unfortunately, the signage, stationery and linens had been ordered under the previous name, and all had to be repurchased with the new moniker. The hotel opened with Delmonico's restaurant overlooking the square, the Fifth and Vine bar at the corner of those streets, Fifth Street Market (a casual breakfast and lunch restaurant set in the atrium between the office tower and the hotel) and Yeatman's Cove, another bar.

Complaining about any change in Cincinnati is a cottage industry in some parts of the city, but Jayne Merkel, the *Cincinnati Enquirer*'s architecture critic, recorded these interesting observations about the new Fountain Square South in 1981:

> *From Fountain Square, Fountain Square South looks new and substantial and rather handsome and glittery. But it doesn't look like Cincinnati. Too much of what was there before was removed at once.*
>
> *What was there was shabby and boarded up. None of the buildings except the Albee were really handsome, though the Gibson was a fairly*

> *attractive hotel. No economical use for the theater could be found during the prolonged fight to save the Albee, and the developers refused to incorporate it. The planners faced difficult decisions.*
>
> *It was not obvious at the time or even during construction how different the Square would look with all the old buildings gone. It is now. And it is clear that too many are gone. Even though the complex is attractive, it is anonymous. It could be anywhere, most likely in some city without a long history or with a history that it has been willing to forget.*

Some longtime Cincinnatians are fond of saying that change never comes to the Queen City, but history proves them incorrect.

Chapter 12

Government Square

United States Courthouse and Post Office

Government Square, on Fifth Street between Walnut and Main Streets, saw its first government building with the 1874–85 construction of the first United States Courthouse, Post Office and Customs House. That federal courthouse was demolished in 1936 to make room for the new courthouse, dedicated in 1939, that still stands today.

The land occupied today by the courthouse originally served as a market place, exposition site, camping area for troops and assembly area for political and sports rallies. Three presidents have visited there: James Monroe, president from 1817 to 1825; John Quincy Adams, president from 1825 to 1829; and Andrew Jackson, president from 1829 to 1837. Abraham Lincoln also visited before he became president in 1861. He delivered a speech at the Government Square site on September 17, 1859. Lincoln's speech was in response to a speech given in Cincinnati weeks earlier by Senator Stephen Douglas. Lincoln was campaigning for Republican candidates for that fall's elections. Lincoln spoke at 8:00 p.m. before at least four thousand people from the balcony of the E&D Kinsey store near the Fifth Street Market. He reprised many of the themes about the future of slavery, the rights of African Americans and the future of the country that he and Douglas had discussed the year before in their now famous Lincoln-Douglas debates. Lincoln's two-and-a-half-hour speech started with his "house divided" reference. He stated:

> *I should expect, it is true, that Judge Douglas had reminded you, or informed you, if you had never before heard it, that I had once in my life*

> *declared it as my opinion that this government cannot "endure permanently half slave and half free; that a house divided against itself cannot stand," and, as I had expressed it, I did not expect the house to fall; that I did not expect the Union to be dissolved; but that I did expect that it would cease to be divided; that it would become all one thing or all the other, that either the opponents of Slavery would arrest the further spread of it, and place it where the public would rest in the belief that it was in the course of ultimate extinction; or the friends of Slavery will push it forward until it becomes alike lawful in all the States, old or new, Free as well as Slave.*

Lincoln was more successful in his campaigning for Republican candidates than he was in his forecasts for the future of the nation. The Republicans swept statewide offices that fall.

The first United States Courthouse, Post Office and Customs House was built on the southwest corner of Fourth and Vine Streets from 1851 to 1857 at a cost of $339,183. After twenty-two years of use, that building was sold in 1879 for $100,000 to make way for the Chamber of Commerce building, a seven-story building erected in 1884. This structure was destroyed in a January 10, 1911 grease fire that started in a kitchen on the top floor and gutted the entire interior. The site was then sold to Union Central Life Insurance Company, which erected its tower in 1913. This building today is known as the PNC Tower.

The site for the new courthouse, today's Government Square, was acquired by condemnation for $708,026 in 1872. Congress passed a bill on March 18, 1872, to pay for the new courthouse, and the bill was signed immediately by President Ulysses S. Grant, who was born thirty miles outside Cincinnati at Point Pleasant, Ohio. It was not until April 1874 that the last market house on the Government Square site was torn down—two and a half years after Fountain Square was dedicated. Construction of the new courthouse, designed in the French Renaissance style, took eleven years to build and cost $5,088,328. It opened for business in 1885 as the main federal presence, i.e., the courthouse, post office, customs house and home to twenty-four other departments. The army and navy housed their recruiting offices there, and the building later provided offices for the Federal Bureau of Investigation and field offices for the departments of Agriculture, Commerce, Interior, Justice, Labor and Treasury. The square became known as Government Square in 1891, the same year that the United States Court of Appeals for the Sixth Circuit, which hears appeals from federal district courts in Michigan, Ohio, Kentucky and Tennessee, began to meet in this courthouse.

The United States Post Office and Courthouse, at the northeast corner of Fifth and Walnut Streets, as it appeared from 1885 to 1936. *Courtesy of the Public Library of Cincinnati and Hamilton County.*

This scene faces west and depicts the 1885 courthouse to the immediate right with the Carew Building dominating the middle left with clock tower and antenna. Fountain Square is shown with the trees toward the left center. *Courtesy of the Public Library of Cincinnati and Hamilton County.*

The United States Post Office and Courthouse that opened in 1939 and is still in use as a courthouse in 2013. The Fountain Square Building, which was adjacent to Fountain Square, is shown west and left of the courthouse, across Walnut Street. *Courtesy of the Public Library of Cincinnati and Hamilton County.*

By 1936, the courthouse had become too small for the many constituents who used the building, and it was razed beginning November 30, 1936. It was replaced with the current nine-story structure, dedicated on January 14, 1939. It opened as the United States Post Office and Courthouse, and it too hosted many other departments. The United States Court of Appeals for the Sixth Circuit has sat in the building since it opened, as has the United States District Court for the Southern District of Ohio, Western Division. This building has 485,000 square feet of usable space compared to 240,000 square feet in the 1885 building. Its neo-modern design was constructed in the same style as many other federal courthouses built around the same time in places as disparate as Pittsburgh, San Antonio and Los Angeles.

The main downtown bus depot was placed in front of the building on the Fifth Street side, and it was dedicated in a ceremony led by United States vice president Walter Mondale on December 1, 1977. That bus depot was razed in July 2005 and reopened in March 2006 as it appears today.

The post office vacated the courthouse building in 1992, although the post office boxes have been retained. The courthouse today is almost entirely dedicated to the United States Court of Appeals, the district court and the government lawyers who work in these courts. In 1994, it was renamed the

Potter Stewart United States Courthouse in honor of Potter Stewart (1915–1985), who was appointed to the Sixth Circuit in 1954 by President Dwight Eisenhower and was elevated to the Supreme Court four years later in 1958. Stewart was the author of a decision in the obscenity case of *Jacobellis v. Ohio* (1964), in which Stewart issued his famous utterance that "hard-core pornography" was hard to define but that "I know it when I see it." On Stewart's retirement from the bench, President Ronald Reagan nominated Sandra Day O'Connor as the first woman to sit on the Supreme Court.

Chapter 13

Fountain Square West

Its Succession of Department Stores and the Grand Theater, Later the 525 Vine Street Office Building

The Succession of Department Stores on the Northwest Corner

A department store has stood on the northwest corner of Fifth and Vine Streets almost continuously since 1867, four years before Fountain Square was dedicated. Isaac Rollman, a German immigrant who was active in Cincinnati's bustling reform Judaic community, founded his four-story dry goods store on this site two years after the end of the Civil War. He did well enough that in 1900, he razed his original store and built a new six-story department store, Rollman's Department Store, on this corner. In turn, the company tore down the 1900 building in 1922 and built a twelve-story building that remained on this corner for almost seventy years. The Havlin Hotel was immediately to the north of Rollman's on Vine Street, and it eventually became the Rollman annex.

Mabley & Carew, which started in the Mabley & Carew Building across the street from Rollman's on the northeast corner of Fifth and Vine Streets in 1881, had moved to the Carew Tower in 1930. Allied Stores Corporation bought Mabley & Carew in 1960, and the same year it bought both the Rollman Department Store building and its Havlin Hotel annex. It spent two years and millions of dollars transforming the buildings into a single building and covering the exterior of the buildings with white marble, black granite and blue mosaic stone. A nine-foot-wide canopy extended along both the Fifth Street and Vine Street sides of the building. This construction was the

The Rollman Department Store occupied the northwest corner of Fifth and Walnut Streets from 1867 to 1960. The Havlin Hotel is to the immediate right of Rollman's, which eventually bought the building and used it as an annex. Note the automobile traffic traveling south on Vine Street. This photograph is taken after the Carew Tower opened in 1931. *Courtesy of Cincinnati Museum Center–Cincinnati Historical Society Library.*

first major development in the Fountain Square area since the completion of the Carew Tower thirty years earlier. Charles Burchard, one of the project's architects, stated that the fact that Mabley's was willing to invest millions of dollars on this site was "indicative of the confidence Mabley & Carew places in both the future of the downtown area and in further renewal and remodeling in the Cincinnati core area." Mabley's moved from the Carew Tower on November 12, 1962, into the 300,000-square-foot space on twelve floors. The *Cincinnati Enquirer* passed positive judgment on the building, stating that "the beauty of the structure, inside and out, with its pre-cast walls of wedgewood blue providing a real adornment of picturesque Fountain Square, will go a long way towards enhancing the attractiveness of downtown Cincinnati."

The Dayton department store Elder-Beerman bought all four Mabley & Carew stores in 1978, and the name on the outside of the downtown store was changed. Elder-Beerman continued to operate the downtown store until the late 1980s. The city bought the property as part of its plan to develop Fountain Square West, which it hoped would be a mixed-use multi-store office and retail building in what might be a modern-day construction of the Carew Tower. The *New York Times* reported in 1990 that

> *stalled redevelopment of a block of buildings on the prominent corner of Fifth and Race Streets and vacant storefronts have created a grim image and downtown shopping has suffered. But spirits have been renewed with recently announced plans for a Helmut Jahn design for what has been named Fountain Square West. If the project goes ahead as proposed, a new office tower would rise 63 stories and become the city's tallest building as well as bring new retailers and a new luxury hotel to downtown.*

The city demolished the 1922 Rollman's building in 1991, but it was unable to attract tenants for the project that would have made the effort economically feasible. The city then went to plan B: attracting Macy's (then Lazarus) Department Store to anchor the three-story project, which would also include room for Tiffany & Company, a clothing store and an outpost of the Palomino restaurant chain overlooking the square. In 2013, demand for downtown living has been undergoing an enormous surge, and the city is mulling over plans of whether to build housing units in a tower above this retail complex.

The Grand Opera House and the 525 Vine Street Office Building

Today, the 525 Vine Street office building sits immediately north of the Macy's Department Store and immediately south of the now vacant Terrace Plaza Hotel. But the office building is a relatively new interloper on the block, open since 1984. From 1853 until 1983, the space underneath this building saw three different buildings that served as meeting space, a college, an opera house and, lastly, a movie theater.

In 1853, the area surrounding the Fifth Street Market was rundown and away from the central business district, which was principally on Third Street. That same year the Catholic Church built a building on 529 Vine Street to run an operation it called the Catholic Institute. The 1853 building's most notable feature was a large auditorium that became known as Mozart's Hall. In 1860, as a branch of the institute, the church started a polytechnic college in the building. Many large meetings were held in the large auditorium separate and apart from the college. For example, when it was learned that the Union soldiers stationed in Charleston Harbor at Fort Sumter were fired upon by Confederate troops in April 1861, a patriotic mass meeting was held in Mozart's Hall. Among the attendees that day was Rutherford B. Hayes, who urged defense of the Union. Hayes would later become Ohio governor and United States president, and as governor, he would have a speaking role at the October 1871 dedication of the fountain. Archbishop Purcell perceived that a large group of influential Catholics was against continuation of the Catholic Institute and the polytechnical college. On May 12, 1867, he proclaimed that venture to be a "grand failure." The property was sold to David Sinton (1808–1900).

Sinton was born in Ireland and immigrated to America with his family at the age of three when they moved to Pittsburgh, Pennsylvania. He made his fortune in the manufacture of iron; his furnaces were located in Lawrence County, Ohio. He could see the Civil War coming, and in response, he stockpiled pig iron. When the war finally came, he was able to sell his manufactures at prices that greatly exceeded what they were fetching in the prewar period. Sinton eventually bought and made his home in the Longworth mansion at Pike and Fourth Streets. In his will he gave this property to his daughter, Anna Sinton Taft, who married Charles Phelps Taft, editor of the *Cincinnati Times-Star* and brother of William Howard Taft. At his death, Sinton left his $20 million estate (about equal to $500 million today) to his daughter; he was Ohio's richest man at the time.

The Grand Opera House was on the west side of Vine Street just north of the Rollman Department Store on the northwest corner of Fifth and Vine Streets. A predecessor opera house was built by industrialist David Sinton in 1875, but it was destroyed by fire in 1901. This version of the opera house operated from 1902 until 1938, when it was demolished to make way for the Grand Theater. The theater lasted until 1983, when it was razed to make room for the 525 Vine office building. *Courtesy of Don Prout.*

In place of the Catholic Institute, Sinton built the historic Grand Opera House on Vine Street at Opera Place, which opened in 1875. The original building was destroyed by fire in 1901. It was rebuilt and reopened in 1902. With the advent of moving pictures, it began to show movies in the early 1900s. The 1902 building, now owned by the Charles Phelps Taft Trust, was demolished in 1938 to make room for the new Grand Theater, seating 1,500 patrons, which was designed for movies instead of live shows. In 1969, the Charles Phelps Taft Memorial Fund sold the theater to the Standard Federal Savings and Loan Association. The savings and loan decided not to renew the lease for the theater in June 1975. A spokesman for the theater company announced that "the intent is the Grand Theater will close. The reason is the lease is expiring and the owners of the property are exploring the possibility of creating a semi–high rise structure in its place. They have had architects looking at the place for six months now." The savings and loan took its time with its plans, and it eventually gutted the building in 1980 for expansion of its offices next door.

Times continued to change. The 1964 master plan for the city called for the theater space to be turned into a new office tower, and this was done beginning in 1983. P.R. Duke and Associates bought the Gateway Federal

The northwest corner of Fifth and Vine Streets looking north along Vine Street in 2013. Macy's Department Store and Tiffany & Co. are on the left, and the 525 Vine office building is to the right. Both buildings front Fountain Square. *Courtesy of the author.*

property (Standard had become Gateway Federal Savings and Loan by then) and demolished it in April 1983 to make room for the new 525 Vine Street office building. The *Enquirer* pronounced that the Duke efforts meant that "the 1964 [Cincinnati master] plan—amazingly for a city of its kind—has finally been realized." Duke, the owner and developer, broke ground on the $40 million office tower on June 2, 1983. The twenty-three-story building, which has about 490,000 square feet of space, has only an 84½-foot lot fronting Vine Street. The *Cincinnati Post's* architectural writer described the building's appearance thusly: "The shoulder, or southeast corner, of 525 Vine faces Fountain Square. The windows in the shoulder form a giant corner. Larger windows on the building's upper east and south sides are grouped to form a wing spread pattern as viewed from Fountain Square." 525 Vine was the last of the major new commercial buildings to be completed around the square, and it opened in December 1984. For its first twenty years, the office tower had no street access—the only means of ingress was through the second-level skywalk across Vine Street. This changed during the 2005–6 renovation of Fountain Square when this portion of the skyway over Vine Street was removed and the building owners opened a new street-level entrance to the tower.

Chapter 14

THE TRACTION BUILDING AND MERCANTILE LIBRARY

At the southeast corner of Fountain Square stands the Traction Building, known now as the Tri-State Building, a fifteen-story office building designed by D.H. Burnham and Company that was built in 1903. It is one of the few surviving old skyscrapers in the Midwest, and it is designed in a neoclassical style. The building has always had first-floor retail space and office space with the remaining fourteen stories rented largely by lawyers, doctors and other professionals. A plaque on the north end of the building notes: "From a platform erected on this site President John F. Kennedy made a speech on October 8, 1962." The speech was given just thirteen months before his assassination. The Tri-State Building, the Carew Tower on the southwest corner of the square and the U.S. Courthouse are the only three neighboring buildings of the square to have seen all three versions of Fountain Square.

Next to the Tri-State Building stands the twelve-story Mercantile Library Building, which was also built in 1903 to house the Mercantile Library. The building is on the site of the public square that was part of the city's street grid drawn up by Israel Ludlow in 1789. This square was to be used for religious, governmental and educational purposes. (See Chapter 1.) The Lancaster Seminary was opened on this site in 1816, and it operated here until 1820, when the Cincinnati College and Medical College of Ohio were established in the building to offer medical and law courses. The college gave courses on this site until 1845. Thereafter, only the law school operated here until it later merged with the University of Cincinnati.

The Traction Building was designed by Daniel Burnham and opened in 1903. Retail space is on the first floor with room for offices in the fourteen floors above. This depiction is from before 1912 when the Gibson Hotel at the bottom right was destroyed by fire. It was rebuilt to be a twelve-story hotel later that year. *From the library of the author.*

Opposite: This 1908 photograph shows the twelve-story Mercantile Library Building at the center and the Traction Building slightly to the north, facing north on Walnut Street. Note the electric streetcars, early vintage automobiles and horse-drawn carriages on the street. *From the library of the author.*

Cincinnati had no public library at its founding, and forty-five men, including future president William Henry Harrison, founded the Mercantile Library on April 18, 1835, "for the purpose of establishing a Library and Reading Room, to be appropriated to the use of young men engaged solely in mercantile pursuits." The Mercantile Library was a subscription library at its start, and it has remained so throughout its 178-year history. The original library was on Main Street, near Pearl Street. The library moved to

This 2013 photograph shows the same view as the previous photograph, again looking north on Walnut Street, with the Mercantile Library Building at the center. *Courtesy of the author.*

the present site in 1840 when it moved into the Cincinnati College building. This building burned down on January 19, 1845.

A new building was constructed on the same site, and the Mercantile Library was given a ten-thousand-year lease. By 1860, the library was able to boast 3,327 members. This building, too, burned down on October 20, 1869, and another building arose on this site. This building had become outdated by 1902, and it was purposefully demolished to make way for the current building finished the next year. The Mercantile Library has been on the eleventh floor of the building since 1903, and it uses the twelfth floor off and on (currently on) as a lecture hall and event space. Today, there are a variety of lecture series, book discussion groups and other events dedicated to good, new, old and wonderful books. The Mercantile Library proclaims: "To fulfill its mission as the literary center of the region, the Library maintains and expands its historic collection of books and presents a rich schedule of events of interest to anyone who enjoys books and reading."

Other tenants in the building besides the library have included doctors, dentists, lawyers, accountants and other professionals. Among the retail tenants on street level have been Mike and Carol Trotta Tailors and Straus Tobacconists.

Chapter 15

The Terrace Plaza Hotel and the Gourmet Room

Jack Emery conceived the Carew Tower project in 1929 and had completed it by early 1931. (See Chapter 9.) It was and remains today an Art Deco masterpiece. For the Terrace Plaza Hotel, just one block north of the Carew Tower at Sixth and Vine Streets, Emery sought and had created something completely different. The Terrace Plaza, built between 1946 and 1948, is the most important modernist building in Cincinnati, and it won national and international fame at its opening. Unfortunately, its design later became outdated and was viewed as unattractive. It closed in 2008, sixty years after it opened, and remains in search of redevelopment in 2013.

Emery commissioned Skidmore, Owings & Merrill (SOM) to design the hotel just after the end of World War II. Emery was attracted to SOM for its commitment to modernism and also because it had yet to design a hotel—this project would be its first. The site he gave SOM to design was challenging in that it was ninety feet deep along Vine Street and four hundred feet long on Sixth Street from Vine Street all the way to Race Street. The original ground-floor tenants were two department stores: Bond and JC Penney. Their first two stories were glass, but the next six stories gave the building its most unusual appearance. They were encased entirely in brick without windows, which were viewed at the time as interfering with air conditioning and hampering the display of merchandise. The department stores were on floors one through six. The hotel lobby was on the eighth floor. This floor also housed two restaurants: the Skyline Restaurant and the Terrace Cafe, adjacent to the outdoor eighth-floor terrace. Floors nine through nineteen

A 1948 photograph of the Terrace Plaza Hotel looking southwest across Vine Street to the left of Sixth Street. The hotel was a modern masterpiece. *Photograph by Ezra Stoller.*

housed 324 hotel rooms. The twentieth floor contained a restaurant, the Gourmet Room, with a 360-degree view of downtown and the suburbs, and according to John Tubb, who did his master's thesis on the Terrace Plaza, it became known as "the UFO on top of the building."

The eighth-floor lobby of the Terrace Plaza Hotel. An Alexander Calder mobile hangs in the center of the ceiling. *Photograph by Ezra Stoller.*

Modern artists were commissioned to create one-of-a-kind art for the hotel's interiors. A thirty-foot curving mural was designed by Joan Miró for the Gourmet Room. (This mural today hangs opposite the Terrace Cafe at the Cincinnati Art Museum.) A satirical mural of the Cincinnati cityscape was created for the Skyline Restaurant by New York artist Saul Steinberg. A mobile by Alexander Calder was installed in the eighth-floor hotel lobby.

In 1970, the Gourmet Room received the coveted five-star award by the Mobil travel guide, which gave Cincinnati three five-star restaurants. Both Pigall's, on Fourth Street, and the Maisonette, on Sixth Street, had already earned five-star status. All three restaurants were French cuisine, but all three were slightly different. According to *Cincinnati* magazine, John Kinsella, executive chef at the Terrace Plaza from 1975 to 1977, recalled that "Pigall's was a provincial French restaurant, the Maisonette was more haute cuisine, and we were more Parisian-style. We did a lot of nouvelle cuisine. People used to fly into Cincinnati and go to the Gourmet Room for dinner, then the Maisonette the next night, and then Pigall's the night after that."

This mural was commissioned by Jack Emery from Joan Miró for the rear wall of the Gourmet Room. When Emery sold the hotel to the Hilton in 1965, he had the mural moved to the Cincinnati Art Museum. *Photograph by Ezra Stoller.*

The exterior of the Gourmet Room restaurant on the twentieth floor of the Terrace Plaza Hotel. For a time, the restaurant earned five stars for its French cuisine. *Photograph by Ezra Stoller.*

The Emerys sold the hotel to the Hilton chain in 1956. The Miró, Steinberg and Calder artworks were then donated by Emery to the Cincinnati Art Museum.

The JC Penney department store closed in 1968, Bond in 1977. AT&T bought the building in 1983 and bricked over the second-floor windows. It converted floors two through seven into a call center. The company subdivided the first floor into smaller retail shops, and a motor lobby was added on Sixth Street. Occupancy rates at the hotel fell through the years, and there were no longer enough hotel guests to keep the Gourmet Room viable. It finally closed on July 4, 1992, years after it had lost its fifth star. The hotel stopped operating in 2008. A variety of proposals have been floated to reopen the building in one manner or another, but nothing has yet materialized. Among other practical problems, the seven bricked-over floors at the base of the building have made finding a new tenant impossible as of this writing.

After having put Cincinnati on the modernism map in 1948 when the hotel opened, Downtown Cincinnati Inc. president David Ginsburg noted in today's world that "many people ridiculed the building as not being very attractive." At this writing, it is uncertain whether there will be a sad ending to the once world-renowned building or whether an owner with viable redevelopment plans will step forward.

Bibliography

Newspapers

Cincinnati Daily Commercial
Cincinnati Enquirer
Cincinnati Post
Cincinnati Times-Post
New York Times

Articles

Allyn, Compton. "Transformation of Fourth Street Into Cincinnati's Financial District." *Queen City Heritage* 45 (Summer 1987): 2–20.

Blum, Carol Jean. "'A Devotion to the West': The Settlement of Cincinnati, 1788–1810." *Queen City Heritage* 48 (Spring 1990): 2–19.

King, Arthur G., MD. "The Earliest Map of Cincinnati (1792)." *Quarterly Bulletin of the Cincinnati Historical Society* 15 (October 1957): 302–10a.

———. "The Exact Site of Fort Washington and Daniel Drake's Error." *Quarterly Bulletin of the Cincinnati Historical Society* 11 (April 1953): 128–46.

———. "Origins of Some Cincinnati Streets—A Street in Clifton." *Quarterly Bulletin of the Cincinnati Historical Society* 10 (April 1952): 143–56.

Knopf, Richard C., Raymond S. Baby and Dwight Smith. "The Rediscovery of Fort Washington." *Bulletin of the Historical and Philosophical Society of Ohio* 11 (January 1953): 2–12.

Lewis, Gene D. "Lincoln's Cincinnati Speech of 1859." *Bulletin of the Cincinnati Historical Society* 23 (July 1965): 146–78.

March, Mary S. "Henry Probasco and Ferdinand Von Miller Create the Tyler Davison Fountain." *Queen City Heritage* 45 (Spring 1987): 3–18.

Martini, Michael A. "Cincinnati's Urban Yardstick: The Carew Tower Complex." *Queen City Heritage* 55 (Winter 1997): 2–23.

Merkel, Jayne. "The Baum-Taft House: A Historiography." *Queen City Heritage* 46 (Spring 1988): 33–50.

Murtha, Lisa. "430 West Cliff Lane." *Cincinnati Magazine*, March 2011, 38.

———. "Room With a View." *Cincinnati Magazine*, March 2011, 78–81, 190–93.

Venable, Herbert L., and James D. McGlothlin. "Quality of Housing and Working Conditions in the Development of Public Health in Cincinnati 1798–1900." *Queen City Heritage* 49 (Summer 1991): 30–48.

Vitz, Carl. "A Brief History of Lytle Square 1789–1964." *Bulletin of the Cincinnati Historical Society* 22 (April 1964): 110–22.

Books and Manuscripts

Clarke, Robert. *Record of the Distribution and Sale of Lots in the Town of Losantiville (now Cincinnati), 1789–90*. 1870. Reprint, Cincinnati, OH: Robert A. Cline, 1957.

Kenny, D.J. *Illustrated Guide to Cincinnati and the World's Columbian Exposition*. St. Louis, MO: Pacific Publishing, 1893.

Poole, William Frederick. *The Tyler Davidson Fountain Given by Mr. Henry Probasco to the City of Cincinnati*. Cincinnati, OH: privately printed, 1872.

WPA Writers' Project. *Cincinnati: A Guide to the Queen City and Its Neighbors*. Cincinnati, OH: Wiesen-Hart Press, 1943.

Websites

en.wikipedia.org/wiki/David_Sinton
en.wikipedia.org/wiki/John_J._Emery
en.wikipedia.org/wiki/Miami_and_erie_canal
en.wikipedia.org/wiki/Over-the-rhine
libraries.uc.edu/research/subject-resources/business/book_john_emery.html
peterloon.org
physics.bu.edu-rednar/projects/population/cities/Cincinnati.html
queencitytour.blogspot.com/search?q=tristate&building
www.3cdc.org./about-fountain-square/
www.cincinnativiews.net
www.findlaymarket.org/market-history/
www.mariemontpreservation.org/founding.htm
www.mercantilelibrary.com
www.Ohiohistorycentral.org/entry.php?rec=681
www.Ohiohistorycentral.org/entry.php?rec=753

About the Author

Greg Rogers is a partner with Taft Stettinius & Hollister LLP, where his office has overlooked Fountain Square for the past twenty-five years. Greg is co-chair of the firm's Labor and Employment Law department. He handles all types of labor and employment disputes on behalf of employers and has been lead counsel in a number of ERISA, Title VII and LMRA class action cases. *Human Resource Executive* magazine has called him one of the top 100 of the "nation's most powerful employment attorneys." Greg has been selected for inclusion in *Best Lawyers in America*, has been named an Ohio "Super Lawyer" and is recognized by *Chambers USA, America's Leading Lawyers for Business*. (His full biography can be accessed at www.taftlaw.com.)

Greg lives in Cincinnati with his wife, Kathy, and three children: Samantha, Parker and Caroline. He is a longtime member of the Hyde Park Community United Methodist Church, and he currently is chairman of the church's Board of Trustees. He is also a twenty-two-year member of the Cincinnati Athletic Club, which is just blocks from Fountain Square.

Greg previously wrote *Cincinnati's Hyde Park: Brief History of a Queen City Gem*, which was published by The History Press in 2010.